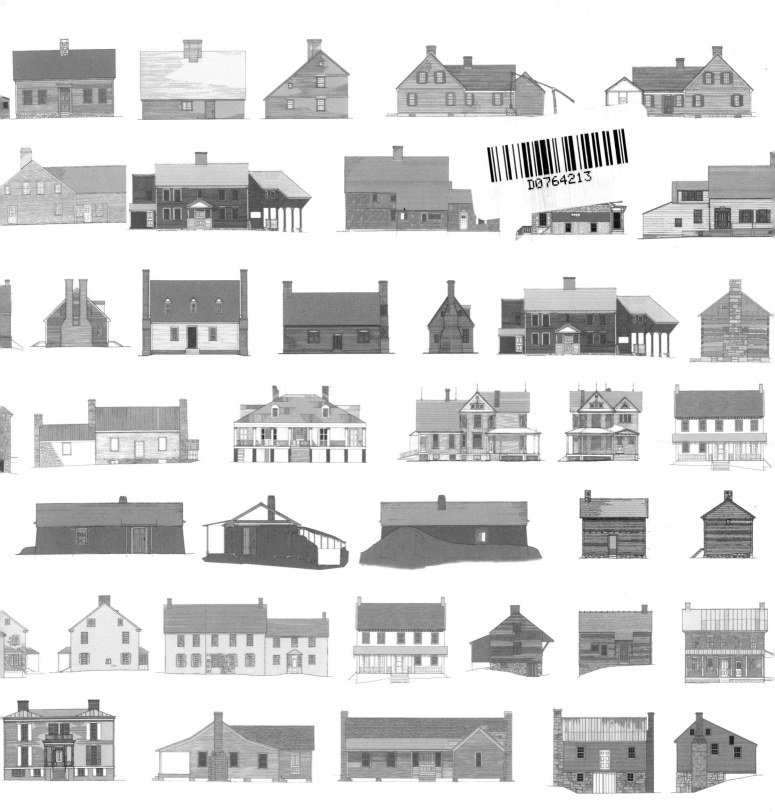

the farmhouse book

David Larkin

An illustrated documentary

the farmhouse book

Tradition, style, and experience

Photography by
Carl Socolow
Michael Freeman
Paul Rocheleau
Jessie Walker

A David Larkin Book

Universe

First published in the United States of America in 2005
by UNIVERSE PUBLISHING
A Division of Rizzoli International Publications, Inc.
300 Park Avenue South,
New York, NY 10010
www.rizzoliusa.com

A DAVID LARKIN BOOK

2005 2006 2007 2008 2009 2010/1098765432 1

ISBN: 0-7893-1351-0

Library of Congress Control Number: 2005904458

Designed by David Larkin

Editor: Tricia Levi

Printed in China

Contents

Introduction

A FARMHOUSE is a building that functions as both a home and as a base for outdoor work. Histories of architecture are full of information on places of worship, learning, culture, commerce, government, and even urban residence, but there is much less known about the buildings that sheltered farming people. There is a difficulty in exploring the history of old farmhouses. Unlike the great manors and palaces that were built to last, farmhouses and cottages have not been as resistant to the deleterious effects of time and climate; however, because they are less permanent and more organic, and are adapted to the demands made on them, they have the potential to tell their own stories, inseparable from their owner-builders. These stories are well worth patient research. This is more evident in North America than anywhere else. As the country quickly settled, humble cabins were converted, divided, sometimes moved, and enlarged into lasting family homes. The emphasis of this book is on illustrating the development and character of farmhouses and the experience of living

in them, and to show how they connect with the altered landscapes and lives of their current owners. Styles and decorative ideas are not the priorities here, although a house good to look at should be good to live in too, but when the function of a farmhouse is lost, so is its meaning. A farmhouse in its place on the landscape does not appeal to the intellect as much as it does to the moral sense. We feel not instructed or edified but awakened in an emotional way; we either want to be part of it or avoid its independence and get back to a more comfortable urban environment. The farmhouse has unity, as every simple building should, and a beauty from the sentiment that it inspires. The best way to look at a farmhouse is to study each detail of its composition, to find the reasons for its constructed parts, proportions, and placements, the reasons for its color and texture, and the impulse that created it. No other builders conveyed with such energy the immediacy of settlement like those of the new Americans, who were enthused by a common vision that was religious but independent of establishments.

What is a typical American farmhouse? The most common type is white, it is facing front, it has a brick chimney at each end or one in the middle, it is evenly proportioned and clapboarded, it has a porch, and you imagine a kitchen ell at the back. The finishing touches are the central dark green painted door, the shutters always pinned back, and a big shade tree. This paradigm is a mixture of ingredients from the Old World. The style is somewhat Georgian, the posts holding up the porch roof are Greek revival, the louvers on the shutters and the porch itself come from colonial experience in Africa and the Caribbean, and the glossy dark green paintwork from the Dutch *boer groen*, as ubiquitous in the Low Countries today as in America. Today, there are slight changes; the roof shingles are now of asphalt, not cedar or slate, and the clapboards may be vinyl. With its best side turned toward the sun it can be identified as prosperous, but the heart of this structure is proletarian or less than that: a shelter for would-be survivors on a sea of grass.

The seventeenth-century farmhouse was built without precedent, with a broad mind: Stones were unearthed and gathered for a

foundation, and timbers cut for uprights and floors, sheds of various sizes, a big barn, and a house, with an addition like an afterthought; a complex, as it were, forming itself out of urgency and the rough cast of confidence. The look of the farmhouse was rudimentary and oppressive, unpainted, its dominating form a huge brick chimney, half the height of the house, the windows small and the shutters thick. A little later the farmhouse itself became more composed, more thoughtful, relating to the prevailing views of the surrounding world, even in conservative New England, where the most succinct emblem of a rural building became the neat and tidy saltbox.

All over the settlement areas of the Northeast and South, basic tasks and necessities of daily life were essentially the same: water was dug from wells; firewood was used for cooking and warmth, laboriously cut and gathered from cleared land; mattresses were filled by hand; meats were dried or pickled; and icehouses were built out of holes in the ground. Many old farmhouse remains have revealed little beyond the fact that the residents had plain furniture and ate a lot of stew. Long-gone farmhouses often did not have skilled builders with the determination to keep the houses standing, although the opportunities may have been there. In the years before the West opened up, many arriving on poorer land did not leave us much more than the stony foundations as evidence of their hard lives. We can imagine that farmhouse: it is small and permanently unfinished-looking, a direct descendent of the scruffy hovels of the British Isles. It is drab. Its shape conveys weariness with its porch stuck on like a broken wing. Its only welcome shows from inside, later, when the lamps are lit and a glow comes from a window under the porch roof.

The chapters and the many illustrations that follow are arranged to demonstrate how the North American farmhouse came to be. There is a fictionalized account of a day in the life of a farmhouse of the late 1860s, when the pace of progress was fast; it may seem almost idyllic, even enviable. Then follows a heavily illustrated section on how farmhouses took shape, how they developed, how they operated, and what it was like to live in them. This section leads to how people can adapt to living in farmhouses today, in the hopes that some of the character of these buildings will remain unchanged and their redundant parts (turned into workrooms, studios, bathrooms, and so on) will retain their proportions and history. The seachange in agriculture and the near disappearance of the family farm have led to small benefits, thankfully; some families reuse these dwellings as a base for new ideas, as places for friends and paying guests to experience life on a working farm, or as places where travelers can stay a few nights in a rural community. Here, the best room in the farmhouse, long forgotten and barely, if ever, used—the parlor—is alive with fellowship. Lastly, there is a view of the farmhouse today, where good buildings, with minimal interference, can hold their own against developers, stylists, and decorators, and can continue to tell us stories.

An early 1900s progressive farmhouse in Urbandale, Iowa.

A day in the life of a farmhouse

4:30 A.M.: The woman awakes in the dim glow of dawn. She feels the space beside her, barely warm in the place where her husband had slept. She knows he's in the horse barn readying the team for the day's work in the cornfields. She dresses and pins up her hair and goes to the kitchen. The old collie comes out from under the dresser, stretches, and returns to the same spot. The woman looks at the big fireplace, where she is grateful to see that some of the banked embers in front of the backlog are still pink. There is lot to be done in the first part of the morning and the fire is the engine of activity. Today is Friday, the main day for baking. The woman shovels some of the blackened embers into the back of the bread oven built into the chimney, where it will be easy to get it glowing with a handful of brush. Keeping fires going had been so important until two years ago, when the kitchen was enlarged and a new iron cookstove was installed. Bending down, she riddles the ashes below the stove's firebox and stacks, and then kindles its fire with sawdust and wood chips. Now to the stone-floored pump room and dairy where she fills a big kettle of water for the stovetop. There is a rhythm to her movements. She goes toward the kitchen door where she gently touches the big cloth-covered bowls containing the rising bread dough made the day before. Unlatching the Dutch door she feels the cool morning breeze and is grateful for the new wire screen above the bottom half. This summer it had allowed the kitchen a flow of air, dissipating some of the heat and decreasing the number of flies. She stands on the boards of the new porch aware that the farm starts at this spot. On the porch there is an accumulation of material that had previously been stored elsewhere: two stacks with logs of different sizes, one for the fire, one for the stove; a collection of barrels ready to be filled

with apples; a large iron pot in which a mixture of tallow, lye, and a little quicklime will be combined to make soap; two rocking chairs that are barely ever used, since it's rare to have time to sit; various tools; and at the far end, a quilting frame. On the way back from the privy, she sees the thin blue line of smoke pushing up from the narrow stove chimney; it looks to be a fine day. It is late September and harvest time.

She stops at the outside pump to splash water over her face; while wringing her hands on her apron, she remembers that the old dog kennel is a favorite nesting place for one of the hens. She walks over to it, feels inside on the straw for a warm egg, and puts it in her front pocket. This will be for the coffee pot.

6 A.M.: Now with the kitchen warm, the family is called together for breakfast, with chunks of a day-old loaf, cooked bacon, applesauce, fresh milk, and leftover pie—everyone has room for pie. Family members eat quickly and discuss the work ahead. This is the busiest yet happiest time of the year, and the kitchen is the center of all farm activities.

6:30 A.M.: Breakfast is over. Left alone, the farmwife sips her coffee, and then methodically begins to work through the morning. The kitchen floor has to be swept; last night the youngsters popped corn in the fireplace and burst kernels are everywhere. She would not sand the floors today but would wait until tomorrow, before her younger sister and brother-in-law come to visit. As she sweeps, the task leads her thoughts to other rooms. Passing the downstairs bedchamber, she crosses the hallway to the parlor. This is where the young couple will spend the night, and it needs to be aired. As it is a seldom-used room, the only one with wallpaper, its contents give her a moment for reflection; the woman smiles to herself as she gazes down at the big rag carpet—recognizing in it the evidence of old family work shirts, pinafores, patterned material, and red flannel—even some green wool that was left over from when her grandmother's worn dress was cut up for quilting. In one corner is the flax spinning wheel that needs to be taken up into the attic above the children's rooms; in another is the harmonium she hopes her sister will play. There is a trundle bed, a cabinet with some best china, and in front of the old filled-in mantled fireplace, a small round parlor stove that may be lit if needed.

7:30 A.M.: After the room is made ready, windows opened, and all the beds of the house are made, she continues with sweeping and dusting, tidying up as she moves along.

8 A.M.: The daughter returns from milking and letting out the cows, excited by the thought of visitors, and she and her mother talk while pouring some cooled fresh milk from the churn into the spotlessly clean pans set on warming shelves; the milk will settle and curdle. Cheese made days before is turned and the cheese basket and press are scrubbed and dried.

9 A.M.: With the chimney oven warm, the woman starts her baking, sliding formed loaves onto the back brick surface with a long wooden peel; the pies and cookies will follow and be placed to cool in the pie safe near the door. The girl throws feed out to the chickens as they follow her and the grain bucket; she keeps them away from the low-fenced garden and its apple trees. Her task is to gather unmarked windfall apples in her pinafore and fill the empty tubs with them, lining each layer with straw.

11:30 A.M.: Mother and daughter hear one of the boys as he returns to the farmyard with the wagon full of unhusked corn. He lets down the sides and they enlarge the pile of cobs between the barn and the crib. It's dinnertime and all three jump aboard as the team heads the wagon back to the cornfield. The girl steadies a jug of fresh apple cider and her mother carries a basket of cold bacon wedged in hunks of bread, some cheese, and on top, an apple pie.

The oven is warmed up for more baking. The fire will have died down before more loaves are placed inside with the peel that hangs on the left.

As they walk back from the field, the woman and her daughter talk about school. With the harvest coming to an end in a few weeks, the schoolhouse will reopen. The girl and her next oldest brother will walk the two miles to school every day. She looks forward to meeting and making friends. She is especially pleased that her young aunt, a teacher at a distant school, is coming tomorrow afternoon and wants to try out the family Speller book on her.

1:30 P.M.: Back at the house, the woman and her daughter continue their work. The girl helps her mother shoo two plump chickens to be killed later back into the henhouse to calm them. Mother and daughter work together at baking tasks. The mother lets her daughter finish the work, while she goes out to the cellar, opening the sloping cellar door that covers its steps. With a lighted candle illuminating the whitewashed stone walls that also support the weight of the house, her eyes pick out the bins that are gradually being filled with root crops. The cellar's usual old vinegary smell is changing; now the woman's senses pick out the new season's mixture of apples, soap cakes, bacon, and the earthy combination of potatoes, beets, turnips, and parsnips. Here too are hams to be smoked resting in a barrel of brine, and festoons of sausages and head cheese hanging from the floor joists. She finds the basket of new mason jars that have made such a difference to her kitchen life; she carries them upstairs to scald them, so they can be used for the canned beets she will make with her sister. Just before snuffing the candle, she stops and sees in a bin near the door that some of the potatoes have sprouted. She pulls off the little feelers and turns the top layer over. She must remember to keep the cellar door tightly closed.

3 P.M.: It is time to kill the chickens. While her daughter boils a pot of water, the woman expertly kills first one, then another chicken. She tethers the feet, firmly grasps the neck in her strong hands, swings the chicken, and then cracks it like a whip until the neck separates from the body. Mother and daughter set the pot of boiled water down on the ground and the woman immerses the quivering birds' heads into the hot water; this will make plucking easier. The long, messy business of cleaning the chickens is barely completed before they notice that the cows are making their way back to the barn for the second milking of the day. This task mother and daughter do together. They spend about twenty minutes with each cow, resting a head or shoulder on the animals' warm flanks. It is getting cooler and soon today's last wagonload of corn will be in the yard.

6 P.M.: Suppertime. Everyone in the household is inside again; it has been a trouble-free day. A new backlog in the big fireplace rests behind the flames of small logs and pinecones. The family eats. The table is illuminated by the glow of a kerosene lamp—so much cleaner and brighter than those that burned on whale oil, and cheaper too. Family members talk about the day and the work they will do the next day before their visitors arrive. Then they clear away their plates, mugs, knives, and spoons. Everyone is tired and takes his or her place by the fire for a while; one by one they go to bed. The man is the last to go. He leans on the bottom of the Dutch door looking out at the night, smoking his pipe of the day while stroking the head of his old dog. He muses that the world is becoming full of inventions that are changing how people farm and live: new steam engines that can be used in the fields, wire that keeps the stock enclosed, and the windows, doors, and furnishings that arrive at the nearby railhead every week. Every time the peddler comes by there is some new device. Paying their way is going to be hard, he knows, but with the two hired hands who start next week they will get the most out of this year's harvest. The unused room on the second floor must be made ready for them. But more of that when he talks with his wife—if she's still awake.

The American farmhouse takes shape

In the late spring of 1607, a quarter of the 140 or so people who sailed to the New World were dead where they had made camp on malarial swampland in what is today Jamestown, Virgina. They had been taken in by extravagant publicity about the wonders of the New World embellished by sailors. The new arrivals were mostly rural types—farm workers, footloose bachelors, and a few layabout gentlemen and their hangers-on. These first British settlers were so inept that the farmhouses they built were pulled down for firewood. One leader emerged; his name was John Smith. He got some of them to rive timber for clapboarding and shingling the walls. Smith wrote after his return to London in 1609: "As yet we had no houses to cover us, our tents were rotten, and our cabbins worse than nought." Seven months later, when additional would-be settlers arrived, they found the survivors "utterly destitute of howses, no one as yet built, so that they lodged in cabbins and holes within the grownde." In mid-December 1620, another band arrived from Britain. They were better organized, bringing furniture and chattel with them. Although they were aiming for Virginia, the group landed in a Massachusetts bay instead. They were made of sterner stuff than those who arrived in 1607, although half of them died of scurvy within a year. These would-be farmers got on better with the natives who taught them much about survival and what a New England winter could be like. They worked rapidly on the freezing ground building shelters rather than houses. In what were to become the colonies of Virginia and Massachusetts, the first structures were hardly meant to be permanent—in the South because the new arrivals did not expect to stay longer than they had to, and in Massachusetts because of the race against the oncoming bad weather. An account from the mid-seventeenth century relates:

Those . . . who have no means to build farmhouses at first according to their wishes, dig a square pit in the ground, cellar fashion, six or seven feet deep, as long and as broad as they think proper; case the earth all round with timber, which they line with the bark of trees or something else to prevent the caving in of the earth; floor this cellar with plank, and wainscot it overhead for a ceiling; raise a roof of spars clear up, and cover the spars with bark or green sods so that they can live dry and warm in these houses with their entire families for two, three or four years, it being understood that partitions are run through these cellars, which are adapted to the size of the family.

Farmhouses of New England

As they began to build their permanent homes, the settlers in New England harkened back to their homes in England—two-story timber-framed houses that were often extended at the back by a typical Essex lean-to catslide roof that resembled the lid of a saltbox. The harsh climate and the immediate and plentiful oaks and cedars led the builders to abandon the East Anglian precedent of filling the exposed gaps between the frames with wattle and daub. They began covering the walls with clapboarding, a treatment that can be found today on older houses in the coastal areas of Kent and East Anglia, and they began creating in the New World a vernacular style of horizontal cladding that Americans to this day are loathe to abandon. The settlers were also used to making the second story slightly larger than the first. The origins for this overhanging feature, known as a jetty, are from medieval times and the reasons for it have been argued. One reason put forward was that English houses were taxed on the size of their ground plans (irrelevant in the then property-taxless New World); another was protection from the weather; and then there was the habit in the Old World of emptying the overnight slops onto the street

below. The more likely reason was architectural, borne of the need to use scarce timber economically in a country where shipbuilding was a priority. The jetty made the building strong: two separate posts for each floor would do a better job than one from foundation to roof that had to be cut into for the second floor joists. Eventually the huge abundance of long, straight timber eradicated this style. But the first American farmers liked the overhanging look, a reflex that persists today on some modern houses to break up boring facades.

More complicated was the construction of fireplaces and chimneys. Although the Massachusetts Bay settlers were used to bricks, there was no lime in the area to make them and it seems that the first farmhouses had chimneys of wood and clay. Fieldstones of every size were plentiful and massive stacks of stone began replacing the volatile wood and clay chimneys. Some farmers had chimney bricks that came from the old country as ships' ballast, but by the mid-seventeenth century lime quarries had opened in Rhode Island and began to serve the nearby colonies. Life became a little easier for the farmers' wives as brick fireplaces and bake-ovens could be built into the existing stone chimneystack.

Above:
The Parson Capen House still has its jetty, pendants, and a studded door for protection against attacks.

The Parson Capen House in Topsfield, Massachusetts.

The Rebecca Nurse House in Danvers, Massachusetts.

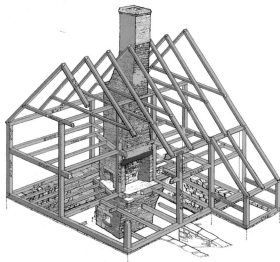

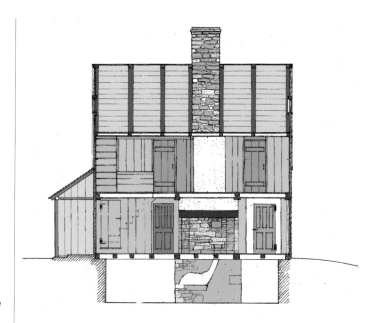

Two views of the Rudolf Trup House in Easton, Connecticut. This steep-roofed saltbox was built in about 1740. In 1938 it was in a very dilapidated state, yet withstood the powerful hurricane that swept through the area. A lot of oak was used in its framing and boarding. The massive central chimney is offset as it protrudes through the roof.

Looking up the chimney of the Casey Farmhouse in Rhode Island.

An unusual upstairs oven in the attic of a house in South Hadley, Massachusetts.

American colonial saltbox farmhouses were first seen in New England. Saltboxes are frame houses with two stories in front and one in back, having a pitched roof with unequal sides—being short and high in front, and long and low in the back. The front of the house is flat and the rear roof line is steeply sloped. The sturdy central chimney is a simple but effective focal point. The simplicity and strength of this design, first seen around 1650, continues to make saltbox houses popular today.

Three views of the Josiah Day House in West Springfield, Massachusetts, which was rebuilt with bricks in 1754. It remained in the Day family for over 150 years until 1903, when it became one of New England's first house museums.

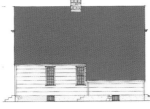

A view of the Benjamin Sturgis House in Fairfield, Connecticut, built in 1720. This saltbox was moved from the Old Post Road to a different location in the area in 1920. In the early 1800s, the front and back began to be painted white. The interior was said to have fine fireplaces and woodwork.

Three views of the John Osborn House in Southport, Connecticut, built in 1772 and left undisturbed when the British burned Fairfield in 1779. The two-and-a-half story timber-framed farmhouse was built on stone foundations with a brick chimney, clapboarded exterior walls, and a shingled roof.

The Kent Healy House, Middlesex County, Connecticut, built between 1775 and 1800.

The Cape Cod house is the simplest of all New England colonial farmhouses. Generally, a Cape is a rectangular frame house (usually shingled or clapboarded) with a straight, unadorned ridge roof, and a massive chimney centrally located in line with the front entrance. The door opens onto a tiny entrance hall. The interior began as two rooms, one room deep, but later Capes often were expanded at the sides and back. The type developed from the last quarter of the seventeenth century to about 1830, and later enjoyed a resurgence in post-World War II America. The wide appeal of the Cape Cod cottage makes it one of the best-known forms of traditional American architecture.

Two views of the Jonathan Kendrick House in Barnstable, Massachusetts, built in 1792.

Two views of the Old Joe Herrick House, Franklin County, Massachusetts, built in 1775.

This is a section of the Comfort Starr House in Guilford, Connecticut. The building dates from 1645 and is the second oldest building in the state. Like other old houses in the area it has a stone chimney. The oak-framed structure had its summer beams chamfered, and the posts have molded lambs' tongues. Just like the first shelters at Plimoth, the spaces between the outside studs were filled with a mixture of mud and grass.

The Jennie Sampson House, North Chatham, Massachusetts, built between 1730 and 1770.

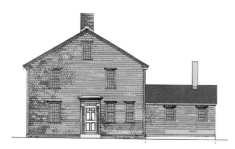

Two views of the Carll Homestead, Suffolk County, New York, built in 1740.

Two views of the Old Oaken Bucket House, Plymouth County, Massachusetts, built in 1835 with a section that dates from 1675. Samuel Woodworth, wrote his famous 1817 poem after which the farmhouse is now named, evoking the memories of when he was a boy working on the family farm. The original well with its sweep is still part of the farmstead now cared for by the Scituate Historical Society.

The Salmon Dutton House was originally built in 1781 in Cavendish, Vermont. In the late 1940s it was given to the Vermont Historical Society and then moved to the Shelburne Museum. The farmhouse is said to be haunted by the benign ghost of Mr. Dutton. The building has a one-and-a-half story ell built at seventy-five degrees from the main structure.

The back of the Bidwell House in Monterey, Massachusetts, seen from its vegetable garden. This immaculately preserved saltbox, circa 1750, is open to the public in the summer and autumn.

The Coffin House in Newbury, Massachusetts, built in 1654 and extended over the years.

The Daniel Webster birthplace in Franklin, New Hampshire, built in about 1780. Much of this historic small Cape-style farmhouse is still original despite having been moved several times.

The Allen House in Deerfield, Massachusetts, built in 1720. In contrast to other saltbox houses, the lean-to here is less steeply pitched.

The Thomas Lee House in Niantic, Connecticut, built in about 1660. The original house is the left half of the present structure, and makes the facade slightly asymmetrical.

Two views of a shingled farmhouse in Suffolk County, New York. Both prongs of the geographical fork at the eastern end of Long Island were settled by New Englanders.

The remarkable hip-roofed Casey Farmhouse in Saunderstown, Rhode Island, was built in about 1750. The house was conceived as a whole, contrasting with the tradition of adding rooms over time as the need for them arose. See page 20 for a detail of the inside of its chimney.

A well-cared-for shingled farmhouse in the style of southern New England.

This five-bay English-framed farmhouse in Suffolk County, New York, was built in 1780 by settlers from New England.

Longstreet Farmhouse in Holmdel, New Jersey, started out as a two-room cottage in 1775. The large two-story house was built in about 1800, and the kitchen and Greek revival porch were added in the 1840s.

Farmhouses of New Netherland

By the 1650s the Dutch settlers had developed New Netherland into an area roughly the size of present-day Massachusetts, but running south to north on both sides of the Hudson River Valley. Unlike New England, only half the population could claim to be from the mother country; the rest, reflecting a more open attitude toward neighbors, were

A typical barnhouse as seen today on a working farm in the Netherlands. The living area is to the right of the chimney.

Scandinavian, German, English, Belgian, and French. But a regional culture developed and this was reflected in the look of its farmhouses, which followed English proportions but with predominately Dutch touches. The Dutch settlers built their houses of wood, brick, or stone in different areas but often used all three materials in one house, making those that have survived very attractive with many interesting details. The Dutch preferred the external appearance of stone and brick; their brickwork was especially fine, with intricate bonding and a variety of colors and textures. The timber framing of New Netherland homes was similar to that in nearby New England,

although the Dutch settlers preferred to support the second floor with heavy exposed joists. One thing they brought, but didn't build for long, was the barnhouse. In the flatlands of northern Europe, the silhouette of the house and barn combined is still common, but it's an Old World shape that did not survive on the North American landscape. The Hudson Valley does not have any original barnhouses. There is architectural evidence that some were built. One of them near Albany, made of brick, is mentioned in a document from 1643; the document cites an agreement for a farmhouse to be erected 120 by 20 feet and divided with 80 feet as a barn and 40 feet as a dwelling. And earlier, Kiliaen van Rensselaer reported that in 1631 the settlers in his patroonship of Rensselaerswyck had established two farms; on one they built a "brick house, eighty feet long, the threshing floor twenty-five feet wide and the beams twelve feet high, up to the ceiling." The reference to a large threshing floor within a farmhouse suggests that it was a combined barn and dwelling. Perhaps it was the abundant land and timber, so different from crowded Holland, that changed the old attitudes about barnhouses. In *The Dutch-*

American Farm, David Steven Cohen quotes an account from a traveler in the northern Hudson Valley, who describes the farmhouses north of Albany:

The houses hereabouts are generally built of beams of unburnt bricks dried by the sun and the air. The beams are first erected, and upon them a gable with two walls, and the spars. The wall on the gable is made of nothing but boards. The roof is covered with shingles or fir. They make the walls of unburnt bricks, between the beams, to keep the rooms warmer; and that they might not easily be destroyed by rain and air they are covered with boards on the outside. There is generally a cellar beneath the houses.

Farther down the river, the Dutch farmhouses were built of fieldstone, and at the mouth of the Hudson timber framing was predominately chosen, but up and down the whole Dutch settlement area there was often a very happy mixture of wood, brick, and stone. There was one difference: in northern New Jersey, and southern New York, including western Long Island, the farmhouse roof often had an elegant curve as it swept down and out, flaring into an eave that projected at least two feet over the walls. This was once thought to have been a distinctive invention of the settlers until it was discovered that the design was influenced by builders arriving from the Flemish lowlands, who had for years used it to protect clay and straw masonry. The look was so popular, evoking a sense of shelter, that the projection was often extended to become a porch. And when the angles of an English gambrel were added, a unique American profile was created: a roof with the downward motion of a gull's wings.

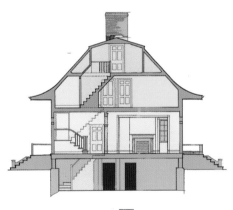

Three views of the Johannes van Nuys Homestead in Flatbush, Brooklyn, built in the early 1800s. By 1909, when the area was being rapidly developed, the farmhouse was saved when it became the clubhouse of a surrounding golf course. At that time it was noted that the original exterior wall shingles were still in place, protected over the years by many coats of paint. The interior was shown to have a remarkably high standard of craftsmanship and design.

The Captain John Huyler Homestead in Cresskill, New Jersey, built between 1770 and 1805. The farmhouse foundation and walls were built of local sandstone, and the exterior was covered later with wood shingles.

The Brandt-Headley Farmhouse in Union County, New Jersey. The original early-1700s farmhouse is the small structure on the left. The center structure was built in about 1830, followed by the addition on the right a decade or so later.

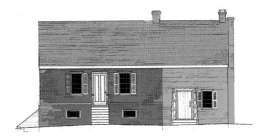

Above and below:
Three views of the Howell Homestead in Cumberland County, New Jersey, built in 1773. In the above illustration, the darker bricks show the original, symmetrical facade, before the new wing was added shortly after. The interior had a fine china cupboard with a winged shelf and curved back.

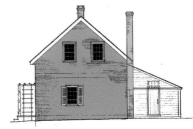

Above:
Three views of the Scull House in Salem County, New Jersey. The smaller brick farmhouse and its extension were built in about 1790, and the taller section was added shortly after 1800; this design was known as a "stack" house, common in southern New Jersey and Delaware. In the plan immediately above, the small original dwelling is shown in red. Note the two corner fireplaces in the later plan.

Opposite:
New Jersey has many examples of farmhouse additions, with timber-framed structures added to stone and brick originals, and vice versa. The carefully restored complex here shows the harmony of the different-size gables, and the typical Delaware Valley style of combining brick chimney stacks with stone bases.

Farmhouses of the Delaware River Valley

The Swedish settlers who landed at the mouth of the Delaware River and moved up its valley brought log farmhouses to America. Whether or not they were the very first is still being argued, but it's certain they did not come from New England. Unlike the nearby Dutch, the Swedes of the Delaware River Valley were better farmers than traders, and with no financial or sovereign support from the mother country they had little choice. For their farmhouses, they adapted the pattern of the log buildings to colonial conditions; sadly, few unaltered examples survive. Log building invites variation. Young tree trunks could be split, squared, faced, or left round and any gap between them could be filled with clay, mud, moss, stones, or shingles. At the corners where the ends of the logs met and joined, there was a great variety of notching—dovetails, half dovetails, saddle, diamond, square, and V notches. The type of wood the farmers built with varied too, so the notches were cut according to the pliability of the timber. Architectural historians have tried to distinguish the differences in the styles of log construction among the Swedes, Finns, and the Rhineland and Moravian settlers who followed (and who were familiar with log buildings) and moved upriver to what became Pennsylvania. All the groups borrowed ideas from one another and were not discouraged from doing so. The interiors of the farmhouses followed the national styles in the layout of rooms and the dividing walls, with the Swedes using the angles inside to build triangular fireplaces in each room. This plan was noticed by William Penn, who recommended that new settlers ". . . build then, a House of thirty foot long and eighteen broad, with a partition neer the middle, and an other to divide one end of the House into two small Rooms." The plan became fairly common in Pennsylvania and spread from there along the migration route to North Carolina. It is sometimes called the "Quaker plan."

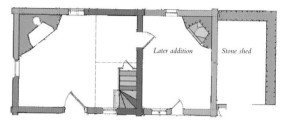

Later addition   Stone shed

The illustrations are based on the records of a Swedish settlers' cabin built near Darby Creek in Delaware County, Pennsylvania, in the early 1640s. The red dotted lines in the plan above show how the original structure on the left was divided.

Below:
The cabin photographed by the Historic American Buildings Survey.

Above:
A log farmhouse in the style built by German settlers in southeast Pennsylvania in the mid-1700s, now seen at the Landis Valley Museum near Lancaster.

Left:
Two views of a small 1820 log farmhouse from the upper Delaware Valley.

Farmhouses of Pennsylvania

There was no distinctive architectural style in the Delaware River Valley until the late 1600s, after the founding of Pennsylvania. The arriving Quaker farmers, with their love of order and symmetry, brought with them the fresh Georgian style that arose on the ashes of the Great Fire of London. The new region was richer in building materials than New England—straight ledges of stone, with plentiful clay and lime for bricks. Joined by Protestant Germans, they soon made neat farmyards that were combinations of like-minded and tolerant ideas. The farmhouses had central doors, framed by classical columns, windows with sliding sashes, and often a facade with a German-influenced pent roof wrapping itself around the exterior walls. The farmyards contained the New World's largest barns, graced with stone gabled ends furnished with elegant martin holes.

The southeast corner of Wright's Ferry Mansion in Columbia, Pennsylvania, which was built in 1738. "The pent cove between first and second stories, and the cove cornice are all characteristic of the early Georgian style as interpreted by English Quakers in Pennsylvania. The long, narrow plan of the house is also typically English and was common in early Pennsylvania houses. Despite the predominance of such English characteristics, the side-lapped shingles, among other elements, are indicative of the local German workmen who undoubtedly helped construct the house." MICHAEL WEBB

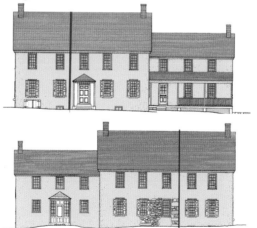

Four views of the Lundale Farmhouse, in Chester County, Pennsylvania. The wall construction was of random brown field-stone greatly varying in size but uniform in color. At one time, a tan stucco effect was preferred to this dramatic appearance, but some stones were left exposed.

The first part of the house was built in 1796 and an addition (indicated by the vertical red line) was built in the early nineteenth century, creating a central-hall-plan farmhouse. The smaller kitchen wing is timber-framed, and it too was stuccoed. The porches date from the 1950s.

Three views of the Slateford Farmhouse in Northhampton County, Pennsylvania. Built before 1850, it is a good example of a central-hall dwelling with a finely crafted, German-influenced interior and exterior ornamentation.

Three views of the Brick House at Willowdale Farm near Harrisburg, Pennsylvania. A mid-1750s dwelling built with bricks baked on the farm, it has a semi-detached stone kitchen. In 1860 a porch, and a new shallower roof and cornice, were added.

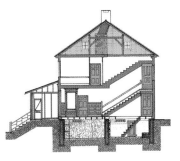

Three views of the Tripp House in Luzerne County, Pennsylvania, built in 1832. One of the few early-eighteenth-century farmhouses where the name of the builder, David Corey, is known. The house combines colonial and Greek revival touches gleaned from pattern books of the period. Fortunately, later alterations and additions were imaginative and functional.

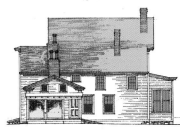

The Theodore Bender House in Gettysburg, Pennsylvania, was built in 1868 on the site of the original Wills Farmhouse, which had been used as a field hospital by Confederate troops during the great Civil War battle of July 1863. The structure has recently received support for its preservation.

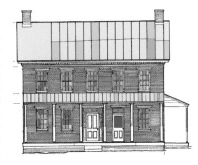

Brick farmhouses of Virginia, Maryland, and the mouth of the Delaware River

The settlement at Jamestown began to exert itself with buildings that did not collapse and resisted decay, and by 1615 it was reported in London that Jamestown:

. . . is reduced into a hansome forme, and hath in it two faire rowes of howses, all of framed Timber, two stories, and an upper Garret, or Come loft high, besides three large, and substantiall Storehowses and this town hath been lately newly, and strongly impaled, and a faire platforme for Ornance in the West Bulworke raised—and further up the James River there were . . . well framed howses, a hansom Church, and the foundation of a more stately one laid, of Brick beside Store houses, watch houses, and such like: there are also five faire Block houses, or commaunders, wherein live the honester sort of people, as in Farmes in England, and there keepe continuall centinell for the townes security.

The farmhouses were built in the same style as in the Massachusetts Bay colony: they were timber-framed, with walls filled with clay and straw, thatched roofs and exterior walls weatherboarded, as in East Anglia. The humid climate was less kind to the posts and beams than in New England. After the arrival of the first slaves in 1619 and in the coming tobacco boom, these first homes were abandoned or used as slave quarters until they rotted away. As more craftsmen arrived and techniques improved, Virginia farmhouses on firm foundations distinguished themselves from their northern counterparts by their great outside chimneys at the gable ends that widened at the bottom to enclose kitchen fireplaces. In the more volatile climate, the brick stacks stood slightly away from the roof as some protection against fire. Arriving brickmakers and bricklayers had plenty of work; there was an abundance of clay and lime from oyster shells. In southern Maryland, the chimneys became positively sculptural, often combining at the gables with intricate designs and bonding. The area around St. Mary's, once the capital, still has many examples of brick farmhouses that have delightful patterns using glazed bricks on their gables. And in the rich farmland of southern New Jersey around Salem, the descendents of the Quakers in the colony founded by John Fenwick decorated their gables with the initials of the occupiers.

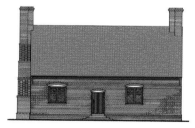

Two views of the Adam Thoroughgood House in Virginia Beach, Virginia. It was built in about 1680 on land granted to a once-indentured servant, and it illustrates the transition from a frontier structure to a more permanent home of the eighteenth century. The farmhouse is now a museum, cared for by the City of Virginia Beach.

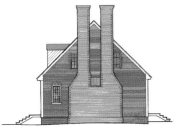

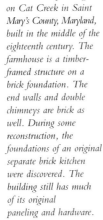

Three views of Sandgates on Cat Creek in Saint Mary's County, Maryland, built in the middle of the eighteenth century. The farmhouse is a timber-framed structure on a brick foundation. The end walls and double chimneys are brick as well. During some reconstruction, the foundations of an original separate brick kitchen were discovered. The building still has much of its original paneling and hardware.

The Samuel and Anne Bassett House, Salem County, New Jersey, built in 1757. The first part of the farm-house was built of brick and the addition is timber-framed. The gable end of the brick structure has an interesting scroll pattern in the bonding, with the initials "S.A.B.," standing for Samuel and Anne Bassett.

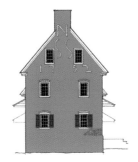

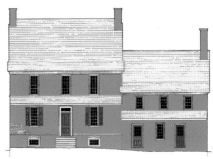

Two views of the Samuel Nicholson House in Salem County, New Jersey, built in 1752. The south gable end bears the numbers of the same year and the initials "S.S.N.," for Samuel and Sarah Nicholson.

The west end of the Hancock House in Salem County, New Jersey, records the date of construction and the initials "W.H.S.," which stand for William and Sarah Hancock. In 1778 their son, Judge William Hancock, was killed with fifteen others when a foraging party from the British army attacked the house. Bloodstains are still visible on one of the floors. For more than seventy years, the farmhouse has been an interpretive museum with many of its exterior and interior details intact.

Near the Hancock House is the John Maddox Denn House, built in 1725. It is thought that the initial "L." is meant to represent Denn's second wife, Leah. Like the other farmhouses in the area, it has a pent roof sheltering the first-floor exterior.

Farmhouses of Piedmont and Appalachia

Log cabins were built in the hills of North Carolina. They were constructed by Scots-Irish pioneers, who were more familiar with stone and plaster than wood, but who sensibly adopted this newfound style as they moved down the Appalachian ridges and valleys. Some of the farmhouses were neat, with logs hewn almost into planks, and well-cut dovetails making an attractive pattern on each corner and needing no caulking. Cleverly, there were downward slopes in these dovetails allowing the moisture to drain. From one-room cabins, the dwellings developed into houses that "breathed" because of gaps that were left when matching rooms were erected opposite. The open space between them was called a dogtrot, and the whole building was covered by a single roof. This type of farmhouse, previously known in Scandinavia, got its proportions as the result of there being a limit to how long a log could remain parallel without too much taper. The individual sections rarely exceeded 24 feet by 24 feet. The Scots-Irish continued building their log homes as they pushed south and westward, first reaching Louisiana about 1790. There they established widely dispersed hamlets and farmsteads featuring an informal arrangement of log barns, sheds, and animal pens and houses placed seemingly at random. By now the houses had full front galleries and often rear shed rooms as well.

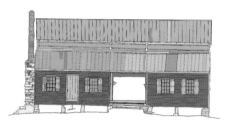

Two views of the Caldwell-Hutchison Farm near Lowndesville, South Carolina. The first of the pens was built in about 1800 and by 1810, when the Caldwells had five children, a second pen was added with a breezeway in between. The roof was raised by three logs to create two second-story rooms and a stairway. By the 1920s, the wooden roof shingles were replaced by sheets of tin. The home has a rich history; in 1975 the electricity generator broke and it was never replaced. Until recently, the owner preferred to draw water from the well and cook on the wood stove.

The Thomas Threlkeld House in Shelby County, Kentucky, was built in about 1815. The larger section is timber-framed and the smaller section has coursed rubble walls. There is a log kitchen ell in the rear.

Opposite:
The farmhouse at the Mountain Farm Museum was built by John E. Davis, a craftsman who took the trouble to "match" the log walls—he split a chestnut tree in half, then used matching logs to construct each wall.

The Peaks of Otter area, in the Blue Ridge Mountains of Virginia, became a working community when Thomas Wood first settled there in about 1766. Like many settlers, Wood brought his family from Pennsylvania, and they constructed this cabin on what is now the Johnson Farm.

In 1852 John Therone Johnson and his wife, Mary Elizabeth, moved into this four-room cabin. The mountain farm they established remained in their family for three generations. With their thirteen children, the Johnsons raised sheep, grew potatoes, and operated a distillery in a nearby hollow. They made apple brandy that was sold to a local hotel at the Peaks.

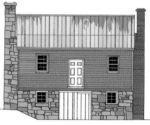

The Sowell House in Albemarle County, Virginia, is a good example of how a farmhouse evolved in three stages. The first story-and-a-half structure was finished in about 1822, and then modified into a three-bay form in around 1830. In 1840, a three-room addition in the rear turned the home into a saltbox. Missing from the drawings is the original ten-step open stairway rising to the front door.

Opposite:
A restored log farmhouse in Madison County, Virginia.

The Creel Cabin, which was built in 1815 in Larue County, Kentucky.

Two views of the McIntyre Log House, Mecklenburg County, North Carolina, built in 1726 by an unknown settler. The walls are of pine logs chinked with mud.

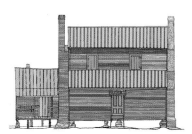

Three views of the Alexander Cleveland farmhouse in Elbert County, Georgia, built in 1791. The original house was the two-story portion with a rear single story added shortly after. The structure was raised with mortise-and-tenon framing and has unusual interior features. By 1980, the Cleveland family was still clinging on to the farm.

Two views of the Samuel Taylor House in Mercer County, Kentucky, built with available stone in 1790.

The Sakulin Log House in Richmond, Iowa, was built in about 1840 with oak logs. When the logs were rediscovered for the cabin's restoration, they were found to be so hard that measuring nails broke when they were driven into the wood.

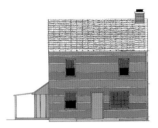

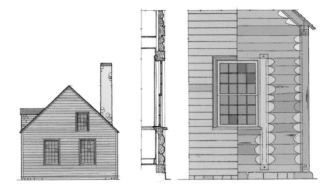

Two views of Quaker abolitionist Solomon Fussell's farmhouse in Madison County, Indiana, constructed in 1832. It is one of the earliest surviving log buildings in the state. The drawings graphically reveal the building's evolution through the century.

The late-eighteenth-century Edward Biddle House, now on Mackinac Island, Michigan, was built of logs with vertical members spaced to accommodate openings and horizontal wall logs that were set between the vertical channels. No nails were used except wooden pegs to attach the upright logs to the sills and plates.

A corner of an early-eighteenth-century French settler's house in St. Clair County, Illinois. The stout building of walnut logs was removed to become a concession stand at the Louisiana Purchase Exposition of 1905, abandoned, and then saved by a group of Chicagoans. It now rests in a Chicago park.

A corner of a restored 1846 Wisconsin log home.

A French influence

Farther south and to the east, the Scots-Irish encountered another way of building; farmhouses there had influences from another mother country, France. The French Creole building tradition appeared in the sparsely populated Mississippi Valley, and few French Creole farmhouses were built outside Louisiana, today home to the overwhelming majority of surviving examples. Farther up the Mississippi, as far north as Missouri, a few remain, but the style was slowly abandoned after Jefferson purchased Louisiana in 1803 and

the influence was lost. One must visit French Canada to see the continuing tradition. The exterior of a typical rural French Creole farmhouse can be described as having a broad spreading roofline, gallery roofs supported by light, wooden colonnettes, and the principal rooms raised above ground. English settlers liked the look of these houses and continued the style, which also moved westward to Texas. In the lower Mississippi, the typical small farmer lived in an unpretentious one-story, unpainted clapboard house where his hardworking wife cooked monotonous meals of pork and cornbread, sweetened by sorghum

The Bequet-Ribault house in St. Genevieve, Missouri, was built in 1793 by one of the first French settlers in the region. It is constructed with walnut and cedar logs. The dual-pitched hipped roof originates from the steep medieval French cottage style merging with the New World colonial porch that wraps around the farmhouse.

molasses, and boiled the family washing outside in a huge iron pot over an open fire. The southern plantation had a life cycle: in its youth it exhibited many of the characteristics of the frontier, but so rapid was its growth that in the lifetime of the original owner much of the crudeness of the original house either disappeared or was boarded over or replaced by a dignified frame house with white columns supporting a veranda roof. Stumps were removed from fields and rail fences built around the arable land, and as planters attained wealth they replaced their rough frontier furniture with polished mahogany.

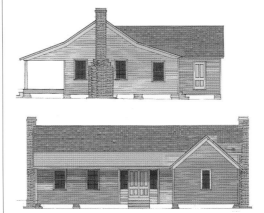

Two views of the Randle-Turner house in Hill County, Texas. The farmhouse was built on what was the northern frontier of the Republic of Texas in about 1845. The double-front doorway under the porch now covers the original "dog run" space between two cabins. Unlike the log "dog trot" houses of Appalachia, it was oak-framed and covered with cypress boards that came by ox wagon from Houston. It has limestone chimneys and piers.

Farmhouses of the Southwest

Spanish New Mexico was occupied rather than settled. People who made expeditions from New Spain in the south were after gold, silver, and souls—not land that could be tilled or grazed. As hopes for precious metals diminished, the huge territory remained undeveloped save for a straggle of often-beleaguered missions. What the friars brought was the method of adobe construction, a North African technique learned when Spain itself was occupied by the Moors. In the 1830s, trade with the United States began to grow and there was an influx of Anglo-Americans ready to farm the land or raise cattle. Many adopted the regional style of thick walls and single stories, and then gradually changed their homes from flat to pitched roofs. Adobe is the use of mud and a little straw to make sun-dried bricks. The use of unfired bricks is known all over the world, employed in Paul Revere's Boston

house and Lawrence Welk's birthplace in South Dakota, but the difference with adobe is in the look: a plain building rising out of its same-colored earth, its surface hand-smoothed with a coating of thin wet clay, is both natural and sculptural. On earlier buildings, the flat roofs were supported by round logs, called *vigas*, carrying smaller poles and sticks called *latillas* on which rested a thick layer of clay. The vigas often protruded outside the walls, giving the buildings a distinctive look. Mud is mud, and adobe farmhouses, though solid and easily expandable, cool in the summer and cozy in winter with their corner kiva fireplaces, were—and are—high-maintenance. If not frequently replastered they become beyond repair. A flat-roofed adobe hacienda with an inner courtyard and great charm became hard to find. The Anglos preferred their roofs to be pitched and they liked porches. The changes made their homes last longer until the new railroads brought timber to rebuild their walls.

The long narrow porches, "portales," became an integral feature of pitched-roof adobe homes. The board-and-batten roofs were abandoned when railroads began to bring in sheets of corrugated metal.

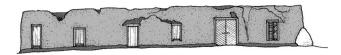

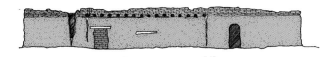

Three side elevations of the Pasquel Martinez Hacienda in Taos County, New Mexico, started in 1804. By 1828 the ranch house had grown to fifteen rooms facing an inner, cloisterlike courtyard. This style, based on the North African "ribats," provided lots of shade. Typically, the sunny courtyard had the water well in the center. Today, the hacienda looks just as it did over 175 years ago, and is cared for as a living-history museum.

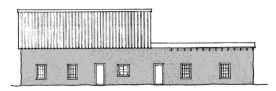

The Trujillo House in Talpa, New Mexico, built in about 1905. This was originally a two-room, single-story adobe. A later addition was a pitched-roof attic that was reached by an outside ladder.

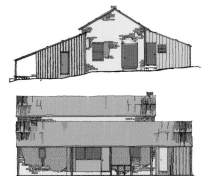

The Warner Ranch in San Diego County, California, was the focal point for immigrants arriving on the Santa Fe Trail to settle in the southern part of the Great Valley in the early 1840s. The building is of hand-hewn tenoned-and-pegged timbers and adobe bricks, typical of the early West.

51

Later immigrant farmhouses of the plains

Gustav Rohrich of Bellwood, Nebraska, completed his sod farmhouse in the fall of 1883. The sod was dug up with a plow pulled by oxen. The blade of the plow turned over the sod into strips about a foot wide and four inches deep that were then cut with a spade into sections about two-and-a-half feet long. The walls of the house were built up with the sections grass-side down.

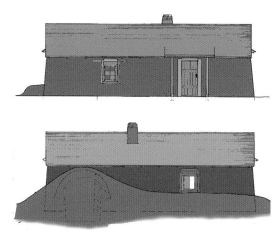

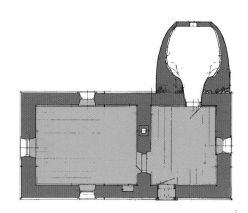

Rohrich built a cavelike cellar section attached to the house, with its base slightly below the level of the main floor; this could be reached from inside the home. The shape of the cellar section was formed with tree branches. All of the inside walls of the house and cave were finished with lime plaster.

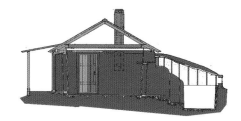

A sod-walled farmhouse in North Dakota.

Immigrants in the middle to late decades of the nineteenth century often came from impoverished backgrounds in northern Europe. Itinerant photographers toured the prairies making a pictorial record of the homesteaders' relatively successful new circumstances, which they could then send back to the Old World. Wearing their Sunday best, families carefully lined up their possessions and livestock to encourage more relatives to join them.

This farmhouse was built in around 1858 in the town of Jackson in Washington County, Wisconsin, by Friedrich Koepsell, who was a carpenter and master builder. It was home to a family from Pomerania for many years. The first German immigrants to the upper Midwest had built crude log structures, but as their farms became prosperous, they acquired the resources to build more elaborate fachwerk buildings, a distinctive German half-timbered construction. Heavy framing with diagonal bracing is filled with brick to form a strong, continuous wall.

This method of framing had been used in Europe since the Middle Ages; it first appeared in America in German settlements in Pennsylvania and Virginia but was soon supplanted by American styles. The great nineteenth-century waves of German immigration introduced fachwerk construction to the Midwest, where it was used for several generations. Proud of their German heritage, on the exterior of their buildings they displayed an evocation of the land they had left behind.

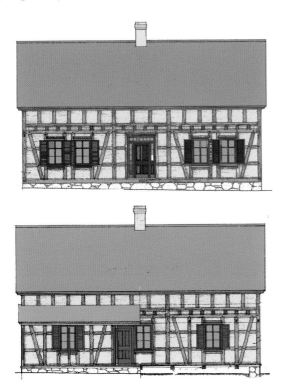

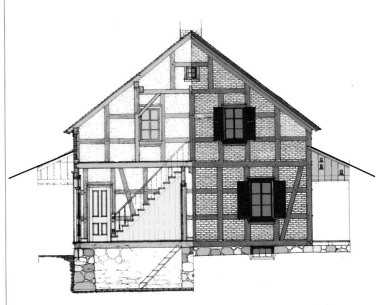

Three views of the Koepsell House. The drawings on the left show the building before the porch roofs were restored.

The dawn of the progressive farmhouse

By the time the west opened up, the settlers often had a choice of what to build. Exceptions were those landing on the treeless prairie, who had to make do with sod until they could afford wood brought by the railroad. But in a country where the economy was based on the growth of agriculture, farmers represented the bourgeoisie, that core of deep change. Farmwomen were often the architects of farmhouses. Since they produced the food, clothing, and necessities of the home, and ran it from dawn to dusk, it was their domain, and increasingly plans submitted by farmwives were published by influential journals. This was the dawn of the progressive farmhouse and farm. If planning, economy, hygiene, and neatness were practiced in the farmhouse, then the effects would spread to the farmyard and beyond. At the end of the nineteenth century, canny entrepreneurs gathered these house plans and offered to ship homes as complete kits to the would-be farmer in what remained of available farmland.

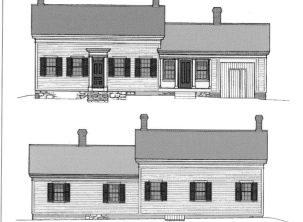

Above:
Two views of the Vanderpool Farmhouse, Waukesha County, Wisconsin, built by Vermonters in 1848 along center-hall colonial lines. The addition is designed as a progressive working unit of a kitchen and connecting workshop.

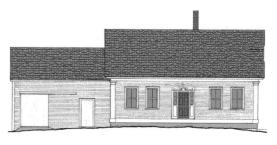

Two views of the Cyrus Eaton House in Orleans County, Vermont, built in 1834. The drawing of the front, above, shows the four later Victorian, large-pane glass windows flanking the original doorway, and the drawing of the back, below, shows the previous fenestration and also the outhouse that was reached by entering the small barn via the kitchen on its left.

The House of Twin Chimneys is the oldest farmhouse in Marion County, Indiana. Now with two additions to its rear, the original brick structure has two front doors. There was no hallway, just connecting doors between three rooms.

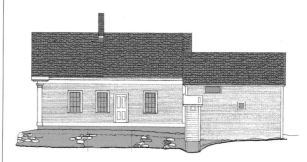

When it was built in 1828, the Firestone home in Columbiana County, Ohio, was a very traditional "four-over-four" Pennsylvania German farmhouse: four upstairs rooms over four downstairs. The double front doors are a distinctive feature of the exterior.

The Firestones remodeled the house in 1882, eliminating the vestiges of its origins and providing a "modern" appearance, from the ornamental front porch to fancy wallpaper and dropped plaster ceilings inside.

Two views of the John French Farm House in Henry County, Missouri, built in 1895. The rear ell was built at the same time as the main house. Research has shown that the building always had a white exterior, green shutters, eaves, and corner boards, and beige door and window trim. The second-floor door led from a sitting room directly onto a porch roof.

The late-nineteenth-century John Mangus Nordin House in North Branch, Minnesota, has had three additions: a one-and-a-half-story kitchen wing in 1898, a parlor-dining room in 1911, and a bathroom in 1973.

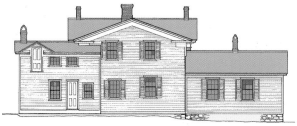

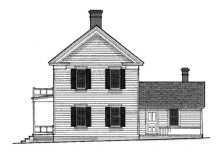

Two views of the Phillip Keach House in Steilacoom, Washington, built in 1858. It was originally surrounded by the many trees of a family orchard business. The present-day owner reports that the second-floor French windows have in his experience never been opened due to the prevailing wind from Puget Sound blowing on them.

Above:

Two views of the Maxon House in Washington County, Wisconsin, erected in 1850. This farmhouse is a typical example of the transitional period of rural building design in the southern part of the state. Its original colonial-influenced lines are somewhat marred by the excessive cornice decoration, but the interior plan shows progress toward an efficient working farmhouse.

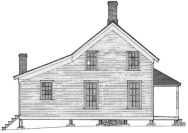

Above:

Levi Hagey left North Carolina and arrived in Oregon by wagon train in the late 1840s. He settled in what is today the wine-making area of Yamhill County, building this house in 1857 after his cabin burnt down. The timber-framed farmhouse evokes the style of Mr. Hagey's Appalachian roots.

Two views of the William Smith Farmhouse in Waukesha County, Wisconsin. It was built in 1848 by settlers from Vermont, who brought with them the New England colonial lines that grace this simple timber-framed building.

Typically connected northern New England rural buildings in Derry, New Hampshire, where the young Robert Frost (the poet) and his family made a go at farming for nearly ten years. The farmhouse dates from 1884.

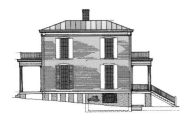

Two views of the John M. Brown house in Washington County, Texas. This all-wood Greek revival plantation house was built in 1855. The elegant proportions are enhanced by floor-to-ceiling windows on both stories. It is said that the moldings, stairways, and other decorative materials were shipped from New York via Galveston, and then by ox-wagon to the site.

Two views of the D. H. Day Farmstead in Leelanau County, Michigan. This appears at first to be a multi-gabled, late-nineteenth-century, Queen Anne-style farmhouse, but the larger scale molding profile and rear gables identify it as, at heart, an earlier Greek revival structure with a Queen Anne facade.

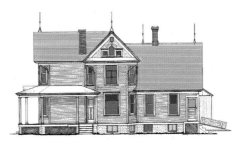

Farmhouse interiors

Many of the ideas about what a farmhouse interior should look like, recreated in today's home-decorating magazines that focus on country style, as well as images of historic farmhouse interiors seen at living-history museums and local historic societies, have been influenced by one man. A retired minister-turned-photographer and "period" furniture manufacturer, Wallace Nutting created an industry out of showing the rural public what the interiors of their homes should look like, and then selling them his wares.

Nutting became a photographer in the pictorialist manner, which was a style that nearly everyone in the late nineteenth century accepted as the main rationale of photography. This meant looking for scenes that resembled pretty oil-painted landscapes or genre paintings illustrating long-past everyday activities in farm kitchens, keeping rooms, or bedchambers. He soon saw the commercial possibilities of these scenes and began to copyright his imagery. Millions of copies of his pictures—tinted, in various sizes, mounted, and framed or not—were sold. But this was not enough for Nutting. Ever the marketer, he determined that if the scenes depicting baking, quilting,

and other farmhouse tasks had historic-looking furniture in them, then they were a perfect platform to advertise his factory-made pieces. The women in domestic scenes eventually became the props to promote the furniture. The more chairs, tables, chests, and cabinets in the shots, the more he would sell. The clutter of all these carefully arranged pieces and accompanying artifacts cataloged a colonial-revival style of furniture design and interior decorating that was to become dominant in the first half of the twentieth century.

Nutting's self-promotion knew no bounds. He wrote books extolling the beauty of the eastern states as a way to publicize his photographs; his photographic prints sold his furniture and artifacts. One can imagine his Massachusetts factory—an assembly line of young women busily hand-coloring the prints while they listened to the sound of the wood-working machinery on an adjoining floor. It must be said that the furniture was well made, for Nutting was a taskmaster and had a good eye, but it was his version of how the landscape was best seen, or how a room should be arranged, that hid the truth. Contrary to the idea of the "country kitchen" espoused by today's home-decorating magazines—a jumble of furniture and decorative elements—most farmers had few possessions, and those they did have were purely utilitarian. Fortunately, today's museum curators who look into the history of farmhouses know from probate studies—executed after estates change hands—that actual interiors were simpler and there was less clutter—more along the lines of the style of the Shakers, who were still making their furniture after Nutting died in 1941.

Far left:
A Virginia Reel, *a tinted print made by Wallace Nutting in 1912.*

The interiors that follow represent a cross section of farmhouses across North America. Following the images of the accurately restored historic farmhouses are examples of homes that have been authentically maintained and restored. Although the hand of the stylist is seen in some of the photographs, they reflect the living history of the buildings rather than the owners' decorative ensembles.

Historically, interior walls were bare or plainly wainscoted and whitewashed. Wallpaper began to appear in the parlors and best bedrooms by mid-century. The mass-production of clocks, mirrors, daguerreotypes, and chromographs in the Victorian period began to fill in the spaces.

The walls of this 1820s farmhouse in Ontario County, New York, are decorated with stenciled designs, probably executed by an itinerant artist, although some might have been done by the owners themselves.

Many colonial kitchens were painted with yellow ocher. The flat painted figure by the hearth was known as a "silent companion." The figure may have served as a fire screen, but more likely is just decorative.

The plain pine floor of the early-eighteenth-century Wells-Thorne House in Deerfield, Massachusetts.

Floors

It was rare to see a carpet on a farmhouse floor before 1830. There might be a homemade rag rug in the parlor or beside a bed, but the floors were usually bare, unpainted and often scoured with sand. In her 1881 memoir, Gertrude Lefferts Vanderbilt had a very clear recollection of the clean white sand scattered over the freshly scrubbed kitchen floor. On the day following the sand scouring, more clean white sand was swept into waves and curves of various patterns with the broom, like the designs on a carpet. A New Hampshire woman remembered that as a child in the 1830s she would draw skeleton pictures in sand strewn on an upstairs floor. When some old farmhouses were restored, piles of sand were found under the floorboards. As paint became affordable the swirls of sand were imitated in a trompe l'oeil manner. Then hard-wearing floor cloths made life a little easier; they were strategically placed to bear the brunt of the muck coming indoors. In addition, they were waterproof and easy to clean.

The late-eighteenth-century chamber of the Gillman House in Exeter, New Hampshire, has a waxed floor.

Carpets did not last long in busy farmhouses. When a fitted carpet is pulled back sometimes an old wooden floor is rediscovered. Today there is an urge to keep such a surface revealed. It wasn't always this way. Until the late nineteenth century, farmers made do with uneven, random-width pine boards that had to be scrubbed and sanded, or painted, with oil-cloths and rugs covering the areas with most wear. As interior woodwork improved oak floorboards became fashionable. The strips were even and the timber was thicker than used today, heavily grained, inviting the use of oil and wax on the exposed edges surrounding loomed carpets. Today, the older, softer, wide pine boards evoke a simpler time and a hand-crafted feeling, but they need more attention, with more frequent sanding, finishing, and cleaning until they are replaced.

Stenciling and wallpaper

The interior walls of farmhouses never seemed as fashionably finished as their urban counterparts. Decorating and wallpaper-design trends took longer to reach rural areas, and remote farmers were not as interested in impressing their neighbors as city dwellers could be. But they appreciated skill and tradition, particularly when applied by traveling artisans who executed stencil patterns on walls, and around fireplaces, windows, doorways, and on floors.

The stencil-patterned wall in the drawings above was revealed when a Maine farmhouse was surveyed in 1967. The faded yellow-ocher background with dark red and green decorations seems to be the work of Moses Eaton. He was one of the best-documented stencilers of New England. In 1792, he moved to Hancock, New Hampshire, from nearby Needham, Massachusetts, near the port of Boston, where the newest European decorative products first arrived. One of these was imported wallpaper, which many affluent families could afford. For those who could not, there was wall stenciling that imitated the idea. In the Hancock-Dublin-Peterboro area there are many examples of walls decorated with the same patterns found years later in the original kit of wall stencils retrieved from Eaton's attic. His patterns, although influenced in placement of design by wallpapers, could not, in their simplicity, hope to reproduce the same hand-painted or machine-produced overlay of colors that inspired them. That is why New England wall stenciling became an art form in its own right. Symbolism abounds in the various motifs. Of those derived from nature, the flower baskets represented friendship; the oak leaf, strength and loyalty; the willow, everlasting life; and the pineapple, hospitality. Stenciling was part of the process of making the homestead ready for a new bride. These stencils brought color and artistry to rural life.

Wallpaper was being produced in America throughout this period, and by 1840 the Industrial Revolution had arrived. Real wallpaper was now affordable for many people, not just the wealthy, and it became a must-have for the fashionable housewife; she used it to cover up the old stenciling of artists. Nevertheless, we are still fortunate to find on rare occasions, under many layers of old wallpaper, the work of Moses Eaton.

Internal shutters in the original paint colors.

Paintwork

Farmhouse decoration was mostly limited to choosing paint colors. A rewarding aspect of determining an old farmhouse room's history is to examine the paintwork. Different eras had their popular colors and shades. Visiting an accurately restored interior of a farmhouse of prosperous owners, which may have purple paintwork and huge green floral wall coverings, such as those found in homes in Colonial Williamsburg, can provide an unnerving look into the mid-1750s. These bright colors are different from the more muted "colonial" hues offered on some of today's decorator charts. Although older rooms often had paintwork brighter than we imagine, we would likely find typical colors for the period and some that no longer resemble their original applications. Colored paints came into use during the last half of the eighteenth century. Whereas early paints were primarily used in a preservative capacity, the basic pigments becoming available at this time allowed a certain amount of choice in decor.

According to Gladys Montgomery Jones, a specialist in restoration:

If you're curious about the paint history of interior woodwork, the simplest type of research to do is scraping down to reveal paint layers. Starting from a small incision, the area of study is sanded to create a broad, shallow crater, the sloping sides of which reveal wide-as-possible swaths of earlier layers. The crater can be examined with the naked eye or with the aid of a magnifying glass with an internal light, if possible. From the seventeenth century on, most paint used on woodwork was formulated with linseed oil, which, when not exposed to light, yellows and browns with age. Early paint that appears to the naked eye to be tan, greenish gray, or muddy green may have begun life as lead white, gray, or Prussian blue. Finishes on plaster are more difficult to decode than those on woodwork. Since wallpaper wasn't affordable or accessible to many people in America until after the Revolution, the walls in the average house probably had a tinted water-soluble distemper paint (known even in its own era for flaking off) or a whitewash made with lime. Whitewash was applied early and liberally on interior woodwork and plastered walls. This was true north to south, from the White House, whose exterior was whitewashed in 1798, to the modest farmhouse, because whitewash could be cleaned and overpainted easily, and because lime was thought to repel insects.

Ready-mixed oil paints were not available until the mid-1860s. Before that, all paints were mixed by hand, usually on the site where the painting was done. Historic ground pigments, which provide the color and make the paint opaque, were made up of particles uneven in size and shape. These were then mulled by hand with a binder, usually linseed oil (derived from flax seeds), but sometimes hide glue (in distempers), a drying agent, and a solvent: turpentine (distilled from larch trees), milk in casein paints, water in distempers. Hand-mulling produced an uneven dispersion of pigment, so early paints had a less opaque "hiding" ability than modern paints and the quality of their finishes was more variegated.

Mineral pigments, like iron oxide, red ocher and red lead to produce reds, white lead, yellow ocher to produce yellows, and some organic pigments like indigo, which produces blues, had been used through the ages. Others represented changing technology. Yellow ocher, affordable and readily available, was widely used from the earliest days of American settlement. But various synthetic yellow

This paneled fireplace wall in Deerfield, Massachusetts, dates from 1743. It retains an original coat of yellow-ocher paint.

pigments started to be used in America in 1781 (patent yellow), 1800 (Naples yellow), and 1820 (chrome yellow, which superceded both).

Pigment identification is key to understanding what the paint sequence is really telling you about which colors belong together in a room. If you found that the first color on the woodwork was a circa 1730 iron oxide red, and the first color on the plaster was a blue—revealed in analysis to be artificial ultramarine, not used in America until circa 1850 when it became very popular in distemper finishes—a lot would be revealed about the history of that room. Without this analysis, one might have

been inclined to "recreate" a strange color scheme that historically never existed.

More recent coverings might emerge. Interiors of the 1950s, particularly bathrooms, had tones of eau de nile, turquoise, pink, and pale yellow, often to match their fittings. Warm colors were popular in the 1960s, followed by various Victorian coatings and colonial revivals. If enough evidence is discovered to recreate the feeling of the room to the time it is built, it would be a mistake to make it correspond to an older part of the house, and make it look older than it is.

Adobe interiors

The Spanish settlers in New Mexico liked their rooms to be a uniform fifteen feet wide with varying lengths. Wider rooms were made possible by extending the span of the walls and ceilings through longer, larger vigas that, before the appearance of better tools, were more difficult to cut and transport to the building site.

Vigas, the round ceiling beams usually of fir or spruce, are a must in building a classical Spanish-Pueblo revival adobe home. The spaces between the vigas are traditionally covered with latillas of materials such as split cedar (called *rajas*), aspen, willows, or narrow tamarisk to form the ceilings. Latillas may be laid diagonally or in herringbone patterns. A family of means could have vigas hand-adzed to form square beams. These beams, with carved corbels at each end, would usually grace a long, spacious room called a *sala* (parlor). Salas traditionally were used for festive occasions such as weddings, dances, baptismal parties, greeting dignitaries, or an occasional fandango.

Adobe homes in this region were made by hand, as were blankets, furniture, chests, and candles. Though commercial wall paints were unheard of during the Spanish colonial period, various earth-colored hues of natural plasters were carefully prepared. A favorite color was tierra blanca (white earth) made from gypsum found in the White Sands area. Its translucent qualities gave walls a cool and reflective eggshell hue.

Above and right:
A sculpted kiva fireplace and an archway
in northern New Mexico.

Painted latillas form an attractive pattern in a house in Taos, New Mexico.

A hand-sculpted "paderacita" (little wall) follows a stairway.

Possessions

Inventories of farmers' estates give us a room-by-room account of their contents: one kitchen would have a chair, two benches, a trestle, a chest, some earthen and wooden dishes and plates, a few spoons, a warming pan, a pothook, an iron kettle and pan, andirons, a saltbox, and candlesticks. In *The Dutch-American Farm,* David Steven Cohen describes a complete list of possessions of a Dutch settler at the end of the seventeenth century as "three beds, pillows, blankets, sheets; a cupboard; two tables; twelve chairs; a churn; milk and washing tubs; milk and beef casks; pails; a bake trough; wooden dishes; pewter plates, pots, spoons, porringers; a brass mortar, a candlestick; a warming pan, stewpan, and skillet; brass and iron kettles; an iron frying pan; a roast pan; a roasting spit; two pairs of tongs; earthen plates and dishes; a Bible; and 'three score old books.'" This inventory supports the view that for the average Dutch farmer in seventeenth-century America, there was a scarcity of material possessions, which, if historian Simon Schama is correct, was the opposite of the "embarrassment of riches" common in the Netherlands at the same time. Gertrude Lefferts Vanderbilt, in her account of Dutch settlers, writes the following:

There were few clocks or watches on farms until after 1840. Most farmers had no means of telling the time; they used the shadow cast by the sun as a guide. The farmwife made a mark on the window sill or on the kitchen floor, which told her when it was dinnertime. A long-case clock that had the phases of the moon on its dial was a particularly useful guide to planting.

Upon the walls were hung tin pans and pewter vessels of various sorts, while the kitchen "dresser" looked tasty and neat, with its burden of blue or brown dishes, plates, bowls, and large pewter platters, each reflecting the firelight or throwing back the flashes from the bright tins on the opposite walls. Although ceramic dinner services began to appear on the

A painted corner cupboard from the Eastern Shore of Virginia.

tables of the wealthy in the late eighteenth century, many of these dinners were brought to the table on large pewter dishes and served on pewter as well. Rows of matching plates were usually stored and displayed on long open shelves of old-fashioned dressers that were built onto the kitchen wall.

This kitchen dresser provides a handsome display of pewter. Hanging from the top shelves is a graduated set of liquid measuring cups.

In *Our Own Snug Fireside*, Jane C. Nylander noted the following passage from the 1913 memoir of eighty-year-old Susan Blunt:

When the plates were scoured regularly with coarse sand, their shiny surfaces increased the level of illumination in the kitchen by reflecting ambient light. Although the rows of pewter plates were a dominant feature of the kitchen dresser, its ranks of open shelves also provided convenient storage for all kinds of kitchen equipment and tableware, as well as a spot on which to put something down temporarily. Usually the top shelf was the only one made wide enough for the largest pewter dishes, but its relative security made it a good place to put something precious for safekeeping as well.

Unfortunately, more appropriate decorative kitchen artifacts are outnumbered around big fireplaces of today, which have become crowded shrines that celebrate the past use of ironware without the understanding of how some of the implements were used.

The *kas* held the valuable household linen—napkins, towels, tablecloths, bolster covers, and pillowcases. A linen tablecloth in Dutch farmhouses would cover the woolen Oriental-patterned carpet laid on the table at mealtimes and would be removed after dinner.

Farmhouse kitchens

The traditional American farm kitchen was not subject to changes in style or character—it was what it was until the progressive farm movement began to compartmentalize the areas of work. The biggest and most important room on the farm, the kitchen, was where everything was done. It may have been connected to a dairy, pantry, scullery, privy, or even an outside bake oven or smokehouse. From this center, the woman of the house would command and control the day-to-day activities of the farm. The kitchen door was located so that she could monitor what was taking place in the working buildings, as well as oversee the garden, orchard, farmyard animals, and the approach of visitors. All this was done while preparing meals for the family and farmworkers, making butter, cheese, and soap, pumping water, and many other daily tasks.

There was rarely time or inclination to use the parlor for a rest. Both men and women, after long working days outside and in, would just want dinner and bed. Parlors were used for special occasions, celebrations, formal gatherings, weddings, and funerals. When portable harmoniums, radios, and televisions first became available, they were considered worthy of special attention in this room. Today, though the television still occupies an honored place there, most rural dwellers have radios and television sets in the kitchen.

The large corner fireplace in this restored kitchen in New Mexico is known as a "fogon de campana" because of its bell shape. The large double-sided hearth allowed for cooking with large pots.

A corner of a Shaker farm kitchen.

Women's rights activist Mary Livermore describes the kitchen of her childhood home in her 1899 autobiography:

The kitchen was my favorite room. It was lit by four windows. Its floor was scoured white, and sanded with beach sand in summer, and carpeted with homemade rugs in winter. It served as a dining-room both winter and summer, the cooking being done in summer in a little basement room made for that purpose. At that time there were no stoves, nor ranges, neither gas nor coal, and the cooking was done in the open fireplace, by means of cranes inserted in the chimney, from which were suspended hooks for pots and kettles. There were bake kettles for the baking of biscuits and gingerbread over beds of live coals, which also were heaped on the cover. There were "tin-kitchens" for the roasting of meats and poultry before the fire—potatoes were baked in the hot ashes—steaks were broiled over hot coals, and tea and coffee steeped on the hearth. The ashes were carefully raked over the bed of coals on the hearth at night to preserve the fire. If we "lost fire," we fell back on the tinderbox, and struck a steel ring with a flint till a spark fell on tinder, when it was blown into a flame. The kitchen conveniences of those days would drive to despair our housekeepers of to-day.

The associations of the always clean and orderly kitchen of my home were very pleasant to me, and are so to-day. My chief delight in the spacious room was the freedom I found there. We could play, shout, run, jump, stand on the substantial chairs to look out the windows, play housekeeping, and set out the kitchen table with our little pewter dishes and tiny porringers, bring in our individual chairs, stools, and crickets, and build up establishments in every corner of the room, and then inaugurate a series of calls and visits to one another, take our rag-babies to ride in an overturned chair, which we dragged over the floor, sing to no tune ever written, or ever dreamed of, till my patient mother would beg a respite from the ear-splitting discord, that "we might rest our throats," cut out dresses for our hideous rag dolls, botch them into shapelessness, and then coax the dear mother to make them "look like something," which she did, hold prayer-meetings, preach sermons, tell stories of our own invention—what was there that we were not at liberty to undertake in that kitchen, if we would not quarrel or get into mischief! Blessed are the children who are under the care of a wise, loving, patient mother!

The cooking utensils in kitchens differed as much from those in present use as the great open fireplace differs from the modern stove, which took its place. The roasting of meats and poultry was done before the open fire, in what was called a Dutch oven. This was cylindrical in form with its inside open to and reflecting the heat from the fire, but stood on four feet. The meat to be cooked was held in place by a long spit that projected at each end, so that the meat could be turned without opening the basting door that faced into the room.

On the pothooks and trammels hung what formed in some households the most valuable equipment—the pots and kettles. In many inventories of the estates of the settlers the metalware was at the top of the list. The great brass and copper kettles often held fifteen gallons. The vast iron pot—desired and beloved of every colonist—sometimes weighed forty pounds, and lasted in daily use for many years. All the vegetables were boiled together in these great pots, unless some very particular farmwife had a wrought iron wire potato-boiler.

A hot water kettle hangs from a crane.

Very little tin was used, either for kitchen or table utensils. Governor Winthrop of Massachusetts Bay Colony had a few tin plates, and some southern planters had tin pans. Tin water and milk pails were unknown; the pails they did own, either of wood, brass, or other sheet metal, had no bails, but were carried by thrusting a stick through little ears on either side of the pail.

The warming pan hung by the side of the kitchen fireplace, and when needed was filled with hot coals, thrust within the bed, and constantly and rapidly moved back and forth to keep from scorching the bed linen. The warming pan was a circular metal pan about a foot in diameter, four or five inches deep, with a long wooden handle and a perforated metal cover, usually of copper or brass, which was kept highly polished. Hanging on the wall of the kitchen, it reflected the light of the glowing fire. Even at the beginning of the twentieth century, warming pans were a valuable antique.

The large, round platters found on early tables were of pewter. Some were so big and heavy they weighed five or six pounds apiece. In colonial times what was called a garnish of pewter—that is, a full set of pewter platters, plates, and dishes—was the pride of every good housekeeper, and also a favorite wedding gift. Pewter mugs were found on nearly every table and were preferred by many who owned good china. Among the pewter-lovers was the Revolutionary patriot, John Hancock, who hated the clatter of porcelain plates.

It was not until Revolutionary times that china was a common table furnishing; then it became more popular than pewter. The sudden and enormous growth of East India commerce, and the vast cargoes of Chinese pottery and porcelain wares brought to American ports soon gave ample china to every city housewife, but in rural communities they made do with earthenware.

The restored kitchen in a mid-1800s Dublin, Ohio, farmhouse.

The early farm kitchen table was long, but rarely more than three feet wide and laid over trestles, making it easy to move when the floor was scoured. In *Pennsylvania Agriculture and Family Life 1640–1840*, Stevenson Whitcomb Fletcher noted:

In some homes the boards were covered with a linen "board cloth." The legal notice of a husband about an erring wife who had "left my bed and board" is derived from table boards. On its surface were round pewter platters heaped high with the stew of meat and vegetables, with jugs to hold beer or milk, with many wooden or pewter and some silver spoons, but no forks, no glass, no china, and no covered dishes. Even the seats were different; there were seldom chairs or stools for each person. A long narrow bench without a back, called a form, was placed on each side of the table. Forks came into more common use after the Revolution, but were slow to reach the farmhouse; food was conveyed to the mouth with fingers, knife, or spoon. People became very expert in loading the broad blade of a knife with food and balancing it there precariously until the mouth engulfed it. Even the elusive pea was conveyed to its intended destination by this useful tool.

> I eat my peas with honey;
> I've done it all my life.
> It makes the peas taste funny
> But it keeps them on my knife.

This rhyme was based on fact, not fancy, but few farmers felt the need for using this adhesive. Even after wide-spread two-tined forks with massive buck handles were available, most people continued to eat with knives. Sometimes a great pot of stewed meat and vegetables was set on the table-board and all the family and guests gathered around it and helped themselves directly from the pot with long-handled spoons . . . a one-dish meal was not considered a privation; variety was thought to be less important than quantity.

The narrow kitchen table in a Pennsylvania Quaker farmhouse.

Food and drink

Michael Umphrey, writing for *The Montana Heritage Project* in 2004, noted the following:

The diet of many farming people tended toward things easily grown and preserved. Salted pork was a mainstay because pigs were easy to raise and the meat kept well. Many dishes featured corn: soaked and turned into hominy, ground and mixed with rye or wheat for bread, or served on the cob in season. Butter and cheese were easier to store than milk, and hand churns were a common kitchen utensil. Turnips, pumpkins, and beans were popular vegetables because they kept well. Green beans were sun dried into "leather britches."

To go with the pork there was applesauce, apple butter, and dried apples. The making of a portion of the autumn's crop of apples into dried apples, applesauce, and apple butter for winter was preceded in many country homes by an apple-paring. The cheerful farmhouse kitchen was set with an array of empty pans, tubs, and baskets, and sharp knives and heaped-up barrels of apples. The apples intended for drying were strung on linen thread and hung on the kitchen and attic rafters. The following day the stout crane in the open fireplace was hung with brass kettles, which were filled with the pared apples, sweet and sour in proper proportions, the sour at the bottom since they required more time to cook. If quinces could be had, they were added to give flavor, and molasses, or boiled-down pungent "apple-molasses," was added for sweetening. As there was danger that the sauce would burn over the roaring logs, many housewives placed clean straw at the bottom of the kettle to keep the apples from the fiercest heat. Days were spent in preparing the winter's stock of applesauce, but when done and placed in barrels in the cellar, it was always ready for use, and when slightly frozen was a favorite relish. Apple butter was made of the pared apples boiled down with cider.

Wheat did not at first ripen well, so white bread was for a time rarely eaten. Rye grew better, so bread was made of "rye-an'-injun," which was half rye-meal and half corn-meal.

For the first settlers out on the prairie, the kitchen was a bare place. According to John W. Bennett and Seena B. Kohl in *Settling the Canadian-American West,* a homesteader in Saskatchewan noted that "We did not have very much to eat. In fact I believe we would have starved to death had it not been for the neighbors . . . who gave us rutabagas and a trap so that we could catch rabbits at night. Mother took the fat off the rabbits to fry our potatoes in and rabbit was our only meat since we did not have a gun to shoot anything with. I used to get so hungry I would eat grass."

At the time when America was settled, water was not a typical beverage for Europeans to drink. The English drank ale, the Dutch beer, the French and Spanish light wines. Hence it seemed to the colonists a great trial and even a very dangerous experiment to drink water in the New World. In Puritan New England they were made to change their habits and to their surprise found that water agreed with them very well, and that their health improved.

The Germans who settled in eastern Pennsylvania found that the clay in the subsoil was good for making their household ceramics, known as redware.

Lyndon Freeman of Sturbridge, Massachusetts, in a reminiscence written for schoolchildren in 1877, recalled the staples of a rural diet in the first decades of the nineteenth century:

At the setting-in of winter every farmer was presumed to have at least pork and beef of sufficient quantity. The larder was well supplied with butter, cheese, applesauce, pickles, sausages, sauce [vegetables] etc. Their dinner commonly consisted of boiled pork or beef or both, potatoes, cabbages, beets, carrots, etc. These were all served on a large pewter platter placed in the center of the table. A mug of cider upon the table was never forgotten. Of this all drank as freely as we do of water at this day. The meat and sauce left of the dinner were hashed-up for breakfast the next morning. The supper was usually brown bread and milk for all. In the winter season, however, when the milk gave out as it usually did in early winter, boiled cider was used as a substitute. In anticipation of the wants of the winter, a barrel more or less of unfermented cider, perhaps made of sweet apples, was scalded to prevent fermentation and used as above. The cider was properly diluted with water and sweetened with molasses. With cold spare-rib or a bit of cheese, it was not a dish to be despised.

The farmwife sensibly organized the storage in the kitchen by having it visible and one-item deep. Cabinets and drawers that cover up the stacks and layers of equipment, jars, and cans were yet to come.

The cooking fire

Until the arrival of the cast iron cookstove, almost all cooking was done over an open fire in the kitchen fireplace. A well-established fire was amazingly efficient, allowing the cook to boil water, roast meat on a spit, simmer a stew, and bake pies or breads. Most fireplaces had a crane fastened to the wall that could swing in and out. From this crane hung the adjustable hooked trammel for raising and lowering the pots. Spits for roasting meat ranged from simple iron bars turned by hand, to sophisticated multiple spits turned by a clockwork mechanism. Other equipment included grills and trivets that supported cast-iron pots, griddles, skillets, and Dutch ovens (pots with tight lids that are either concave or turned up at the rim to hold hot coals on top). You can visit historic houses throughout the United States, or places like historic Williamsburg, Virginia, Deerfield, Massachusetts, and Greenfield, Michigan, to see fully equipped kitchen fireplaces, and sometimes a demonstration of their use.

Cooking in a fireplace is not difficult to learn. It can be done successfully with patience and only a few basic utensils. You will need a grate, a trivet to support pots, and cookware made of cast iron. The most useful for starting out are a frying pan with a lid and a large Dutch oven. (If you have the pans but no lids, use double or triple layers of aluminum foil tightly sealed at the rim.) You might want to acquire one extra item: a tin reflecting oven is good for baking or roasting in front of the fire and can be either homemade or found through camping suppliers. With this preparation, you'll be able to cook great food, even while experiencing long power outages.

First, build a good fire using hardwood, then let it burn down until there is a bed of hot wood coals, which will produce long-lasting heat. Do not use softwood because it does not leave hot coals. You are then ready to cook on a trivet, bake in the ashes, roast meat on a dangle spit, or use a reflecting oven.

A view through the doorway of a detached kitchen in the South.

Fireplace cooking in Baton Rouge, Louisiana.

Using the fire

Trivet:
Place the trivet on the side of the fire, heap hot coals underneath, and put the pot of water, soup, or stew on top. The hot coals will bring the liquid to a boil and then, as the heat lessens, it will simmer quietly.

Above:
A reflector oven is made ready at a Moravian community farmhouse kitchen.

Reflecting Oven:
Usually made of tin, these three-sided ovens sit on the hearth and reflect the heat from the fire back toward the meat or pot. They have hooks or spits from which small birds or pieces of meat can be hung. Alternately, they can serve as baking ovens when pots are placed inside and rotated during cooking for even heat.

The Dutch Oven:
This pot can be used on a trivet or nestled in the coals. You can cook pies, soda breads, and casseroles in oven-safe dishes; to keep the bottom from burning, place a small trivet inside the oven. Heap coals on the lid and check at regular intervals. If the food is cooking too quickly, remove coals from the lid; if too slowly, add more coals.

Ashes:
Potatoes and vegetables with thick skins, like acorn squash, can be buried in gray ashes and then topped with hot coals. This also works for fish and other vegetables in foil packages. In earlier times, these would have been placed in a natural wrapper such as soaked green corn husks.

Spit:
To make a simple spit, tie meat securely with butcher's twine and attach the other end to the mantelpiece or damper handle. The meat should be about 3 inches above the hearth and 8 to 10 inches from the fire. The heat and weight will cause the meat to rotate slowly, and the cook can help by twisting the twine now and then. A drip pan should be positioned directly underneath to catch the juices. The addition of a reflector on the hearthside will help cook the meat evenly. You can make one by covering a cookie sheet with foil and propping it up in front of the roast with bricks, a concrete block, cooking pot, or other fireproof item.

A fillet of beef twists slowly over its drip pan.

The stone kitchen fireplace of a restored two-hundred-year-old log farmhouse in Virginia. On the hearth is a reflector oven. Beyond it the hot embers roast a rabbit on an andiron spit and a fowl hanging from a crane.

Farmhouse bedchambers

The bedchambers in early farmhouses were usually located on the ground floor where rooms could be warmed from the dying fire in the kitchen. Families were large and homes had many trundle beds that could be rolled out at night. It was normal for mother, father, and all the children up to their teenage years to sleep in one area. Studies of early dwellings indicate that bed furniture such as hangings and curtains were relatively uncommon. Initially, the bedroom would be a partitioned area off the main room; later, upstairs chambers as we now know them were constructed. In the Northeast, the upper story was only used during spring, summer, and fall. Even in the larger farmhouses, it was not unusual to sleep downstairs in winter beside the fire or stove, the upstairs having been closed off against the cold.

People might associate historic farmhouses with canopied four-poster beds—and staying as a guest in a farm bed-and-breakfast with a canopied four-poster bed is a novelty for city people and worth a detour—but they were not typical in most historic farmhouses. Before the 1800s, nearly all farm families slept on a simple frame bedstead, strung with rope to support a mattress. However, after the 1730s, mostly in towns and among well-off landowners, ceilings in homes rose above eight feet in height and made four-posters popular until about 1835, when more bedchambers had stoves to provide heat. The four posts were connected at the top by a frame, or tester, from which hung a valance, often matching the pattern of the curtains below. The curtains were an extra measure of draft protection and privacy, making the bed a chamber in itself.

A bedchamber in the 1797 Ebeneezer Alden House in Union, Maine. Note the trundle bed at the foot of the four-poster.

I recall a Shaker room where an outside wall next to the bed was covered with a large sheet of linen, hung neatly from the pegboard, which served as protection against the winter cold.

For young children, a small trundle bed, in Dutch *een slaapbank op rollen,* was frequently used. It was a low bedstead on rollers. During the day, it was rolled under the high-post bedstead and hidden by the valance. At night this was rolled out at the side of the mother, and was convenient for her watchful care over the little ones.

On this page a neat "turn-up" bedstead rests against a kitchen wall in Historic Deerfield, Massachusetts. Leaning against the head of the bed is a wrench to tighten the often sagging ropes. After being inserted through the gap between the rope and the outside of the frame, the wrench was used to twist, and thus tighten, the rope. It required a man's strength to turn the wrench as these beds were put together; someone was stationed at each post to keep it upright, and the woman of the house would supervise this laborious process making sure the tension was just right. When the bedstead was duly corded and strung to the required tension, a straw bed in a case of unbleached homemade linen was placed over the cords, and upon this were piled three or four featherbeds, and even more if this was the spare-room bedstead used for company.

Eventually, the ropes were replaced by boards, making it easier to slide a space-saving trundle bed underneath. The Victorians, in their passion to use industrial solutions to solve domestic problems, argued that wood was unhygienic—full of disease-carrying bugs—and gave us the brass bedstead. For a quarter of the price, you could have iron, with brass knobs. Bed curtains in the form of netting were used before the invention of window screens. These were understandably popular on the four-poster, and even the half-tester, in the South.

Above: *A "turn-up" bedstead rests against a kitchen wall. Leaning against the head of the bed is a wrench to tighten sagging ropes.*

Opposite: *A later "turn-up" bedstead in a historic farmhouse in Pecatonica, Illinois.*

The sheets and pillowcases used in farmhouse bedchambers were always of linen, and the blankets were homemade, woven from the wool of the sheep sheared from the farm. They were thick and heavy and represented a lot of spinning and weaving work. There were other coverings for beds besides the blankets; these were made by family members, by dyeing wool or flax and weaving the cloth in patterns. They were often blue and white, as the dye was indigo. The various intricate designs of patchwork quilting occupied a farmwife's few spare moments. In 1909, Gertrude Lefferts Vanderbilt described bed coverings and bedsteads in New York Dutch farmhouses:

It is a mistake, however, to think that these patchwork quilts, however neatly made or elaborately designed, were considered for the last sixty years as the suitable upper covering on the best bed. There was a heavy white coverlet used for such a purpose, which bore some resemblance to what is called now a Marseilles quilt; the figure upon it was more puffed out, being stuffed with cotton, and the coverlet

This is said to be the bed that Daniel Boone passed away on. He died in 1820, ten years after his home in St. Charles County, Missouri, was completed.

itself was heavier than the modern material, which it somewhat resembled.

This white coverlet was used when white dimity curtains were on the bedstead; these were generally trimmed with ball fringe, and the hanging, festooning, and arranging of these curtains required a great amount of skill, patience, and labor. Another coverlet, much used, can be described as a white cotton corded rep; the design was woven on the surface in little knots or knobs. The bedsteads, particularly those which were in the best bedroom, had the four posts richly carved; these reached to the ceiling and were surmounted with a tester.

Bedsteads similar to these are frequently seen in England, but now are rarely found here, having been replaced by French bedsteads.

A material also much used for curtains and coverlets in the beginning of the twentieth century was of linen. It was printed in bright colors, with an India pattern of palm trees and Asian birds, with interlacing vines and foliage. This material was expensive, but it was very durable, and no amount of washing, or even boiling, could make it fade.

Canopied bedsteads varied in shape; some had square tops reaching to the ceiling, with an upper valance on three sides and long curtains

An uncluttered bedroom of a restored two-hundred-year-old Virginia log farmhouse.

at the posts. Others were rounded over the top. The posts, not being so tall, were finished by an ornamental knob or ball; the curtains were festooned below the canopy, which, springing from the posts, made an arch covered with chintz like the curtains. Cradles were not the pretty, satin-lined, rattan baskets such as those in which the children of this generation are rocked. They were of heavy, solid mahogany, with a mahogany roof, if we may so call it, which extended one-third of the length above, to shield the light from the eyes of the little sleeper.

According to Stevenson Whitcomb Fletcher, in the German settlement area of Pennsylvania, farmers were partial to the featherbeds they remembered from the old country. From the farmyard fowl they gradually accumulated goose, chicken, and duck feathers for stuffing. Geese were kept more for feathers and as farm-yard guards than for food. Fine feathers and

down were stripped from live birds three or four times a year and steamed and cured for bedding. Germans used feather ticks not only to sleep on but also for cover. "They cover themselves in winter with light feather beds instead of blankets," wrote Doctor Benjamin Rush in 1790, "in this contrivance there is both convenience and economy, for the beds are warmer than blankets and are made by themselves." Those who were not accustomed to feather beds, however, often found them uncomfortable. In 1777 Elkanah Watson, the agriculturist of Massachusetts, traveled through Lancaster County. "At Reamstown," he says, "I was placed between two beds without sheets or pillows. This, as I was told, was a prevailing custom but which, as far as my experience goes, tends little to promote either sleep or comfort."

Farmhouse parlors

Just like the formal front door, the farmhouse parlor was rarely used. Originating from the French *parleur* (a place for conversation), here was a room that nobody knew quite what to do with, but it was felt to be a necessary part of home life even though its existence was mostly symbolic. The need for a formal downstairs room seemed to have been bred into busy rural homemakers from every old-world heritage, and in the early part of the nineteenth century a parlor was a sign of achievement. The room contained the family treasures, padded armchairs and a sofa, pictures on the wall, books, bric-a-brac, musical instruments, and some glass and china. But it was gloomy, airless, and shuttered to protect its contents, as the poet Bill Holm said, ". . . everything was covered with little lace white doilies and coverlets, and there were dead relatives on the walls—nobody ever got in there."

Sally McMurry found in a *Cultivator* magazine, that an irritated correspondent in 1855 had a neighbor with a parlor which:

. . . has been kept shut up as a dead property, and to our certain knowledge, has been used but twice in 15 years, once for a quilting party, and once for a wedding. The owner, to have more room, added in the first place a kitchen to his main building, so as to have a dining or living room and "save" his parlor; next, the kitchen was converted into a dining room, and the wood house was lathed and plastered for a kitchen; and several successive additions have been made—the parlor remaining in solitary loneliness. Now if this room, kept for show, and never made visible, with its furniture cost $500, then its use once in seven years, with interest, decay, etc[,] costs about $400 for each occasion.

In earlier times in New England, the formal downstairs chamber had perhaps been more useful. In houses with a massive central chimney and a steep narrow stairway just behind the front door, those who had died upstairs were carried down to a coffin placed in this room. Being difficult to maneuver, the coffin with its deceased would often leave the parlor via a corner door connecting to the outside, known as a "coffin door."

By the 1800s paying respects, formal meetings, and wedding ceremonies did not justify the existence of a parlor in the minds of progressive farmers' wives. According to Mrs. E. H. Leland in *Farm Homes: In-Doors and Out-Doors* (1881):

Just here I want to enter my humblest protest against any parlor that pinches and stints other rooms in order to exist. First, secure the convenient kitchen, the pleasant dining-room, the well-sunned and well-ventilated bedrooms, the bathroom, the simple pantry and milk-room. Then, if space permits, have a parlor by all means—as pretty a parlor as possible—and use it. It is bad taste and bad morals to make "most anything" answer for family use day after day, while the best room . . . is sacredly reserved for outside people, people who are not greatly benefited after all, for when we visit do we not observe that it is the simple, easily served meal that we enjoy, and not the stiff atmosphere of a seldom-used room, . . . and the general feeling that we are creating an unusual and perhaps troublesome stir in the everyday lives of our friends?

So the parlor got designed out of the way in the "new" farmhouses, but it was still there in the older ones and not doing much. It is only in recent years that it has been given a new reason for being and is now living up to its original description.

The restrained parlor of an Illinois farmhouse.

Keeping warm in a farmhouse

For Alice Morse Earle, the true essence of the old-time fireside is found in John Greenleaf Whittier's *Snow-bound*. She states in her 1898 *Home Life in Colonial Days*, "The very chimney, fireplace, and hearthstone of which his beautiful lines were written, the kitchen of Whittier's boyhood home, at East Haverhill, Massachusetts, still stands. His description of the 'laying the fire' can never be equaled by any prose":

We piled with care our nightly stack
Of wood against the chimney back—
The oaken log, green, huge, and thick,
And on its top the stout back-stick;
The knotty fore-stick laid apart,
And filled between with curious art
The ragged brush; then hovering near,
We watched the first red blaze appear,
Heard the sharp crackle, caught the gleam
On whitewashed wall and sagging beam,
Until the old, rude-furnished room
Burst, flower-like, into rosy bloom.
Shut in from all the world without
We sat the clean winged hearth about,
Content to let the north wind roar,
In baffled rage at pane and door,
While the red logs before us beat
The frost-line back with tropic heat;
And ever, when a louder blast
Shook beam and rafter as it passed,
The merrier up its roaring draught
The great throat of the chimney laughed,
The house dog on his paws outspread
Laid to the fire his drowsy head,
The cat's dark silhouette on the wall
A couchant tiger's seemed to fall;

And, for the winter fireside meet
Between the andirons' straddling feet
The mug of cider simmered slow,
And apples sputtered in a row
And, close at hand, the basket stood
With nuts from brown October's woods
What matter how the night behaved!
What matter how the north wind raved!
Blow high, blow low, not all its snow
Could quench our hearth-fire's ruddy glow.

Throughout the farming year, life centered around fireplaces and stoves. Even empty or cold they dominate every farmhouse room and people will gather by them out of habit or perhaps from some deeper instinct. It's difficult today to imagine that in the past the kitchen fire was the only means of warming known, and at the end of winter nights it was carefully raked and banked to ensure its survival until morning. Harriet Beecher Stowe reported:

One of my most vivid childish remembrances is the length of our winters, the depth of the snows, the raging fury of the storms that used to whirl over the old farm-house, shrieking and piping and screaming round each angle and corner, and thundering down the chimney in a way that used to threaten to topple all down before it. Those were cold days par excellence, when everybody talked of the weather as something exciting and tremendous, when the cider would freeze in the cellar, and the bread in the milk-room would be like blocks of ice, when not a drop of water could be got out of the sealed well, and the very chimney-back over the raked-up fire would be seen in the morning sparkling with a rime of frost crystals. How the sledges used to squeak over the hard snow, and the breath freeze on

Opposite page:
In this Ohio bedroom the focal point is a wing chair with early crewel upholstery. Leaning against the wall is a brass bed warmer and inside the fireplace is a crane rescued from an earlier house. Above, festooned for Christmas, is a portrait of an unknown woman by an equally unknown, and probably itinerant, artist.

the hair, and beard, and woolly comforters around the necks of the men, as one and another brought in news of the wonderful, unheard-of excesses of Jack Frost during the foregone night! There was always something exhilarating about those extremely cold days, when a very forest of logs, heaped up and burning in the great chimney, could not warm the other side of the kitchen; and when Aunt Lois, standing with her back so near the blaze as to be uncomfortable warm, yet found her dish-towel freezing in her hand, while she wiped the teacup drawn from the almost boiling water. When things got to this point, we little folks were jolly. It was an excitement, an intoxication; it filled life full of talk. People froze the tips of their noses, their ears, their toes; we froze our own. Whoever touched a door-latch incautiously, in the early morning, received a skinning bite from Jack. The axe, the saw, the hatchet, all the iron tools, in short, were possessed of a cold devil ready to snap out at any incautious hand that meddled with him.

The one great central kitchen fire was the only means of warming known in the house, and duly at nine o'clock every night it was raked up, and all the family took their way to bedchambers that never knew a fire, where the very sheets and blankets seemed so full of stinging cold air that they made one's fingers tingle; and where, after getting into bed, there was a prolonged shiver, until one's own internal heat-giving economy had warmed through the whole icy mass.

Some warmth could be borrowed with stones or bricks heated by the fire and wrapped in bits of old blanket, or one could use a warming pan filled with embers.

Most farmhouses were sited so that they faced south to get some warmth from the sun. Stone or brick buildings were cooler than wooden ones and needed insulation; in coastal New England seaweed was used inside the walls. In the Northeast, big central chimneys with fireplaces opening into each room gave out some warmth, and the low ceilings helped as well. Indoor shutters in unused rooms were kept fastened, and all sorts of materials were placed on thresholds and windowsills to keep out the drafts. One tip pointed out by Jane C. Nylander, from *Eliza Leslie's House Book,* was to "keep the key always in the lock."

Although inefficient as a source of home heating, the large farm kitchen hearth was where the farmer's wife operated a controllable fire which roasted and toasted food. Boiling and stewing pots were hung over a small flame. To use more of the fire's energy some coals were moved underneath Dutch ovens or into the deep hole of the bread oven.

The key to keeping the fire going all day was how it was set. At the back of the andirons was placed the biggest available slow-burning log, preferably unseasoned hickory, and in front another log, smaller but just as wide, known as the forestick. In between the fire was kindled and then added to during the day.

Wallace Nutting and decorators following his "photographs of early farm interiors" overpopulated the fireplace with iron cranes, lugpoles, hooks, trammels, kettles, tongs, and pokers. The actual arrangement was spare and the successful technique of fireplace cooking depended on the resourcefulness of the cook. Farmhouse rooms in winter only began to get cozy after the clever Benjamin Franklin invented his warming stove and Benjamin Thompson, also known as Count Rumford, redesigned the fireplace. This was the end of the hearth with an inglenook large enough to sit inside. The Rumford fireplace was an extraordinary success. Previously drafty chimney throats were so large that chimney-sweep boys clambered inside to clean them. Thompson suggested that a fireplace that was shallow in depth with a curved, narrow smoke shelf in the chimney opening would let no smoke into the room, be more effective in controlling drafts, and radiate much more heat. Importantly, the sides were angled so that the radiant heat would be reflected out into the room rather than stay in the fireplace or go up the chimney. The proportions were simple and are followed to this day by masons who know that the design meets stringent emissions standards: the height and the width of the opening is three times the depth of the firebox.

Above:
A side elevation of Count Rumford's original design.

Center left:
A version of an angled fireplace in an Ontario County, New York, bedchamber. Note the trundle bed.

Below:
A modern working Rumford fireplace.

Using the fireplace

Early fall is a good time to get your pile of kindling ready for the winter. Small pieces of kindling wood will ignite quickly and help get hardwood logs burning. You can walk around your field and pick up dry tree limbs and sticks that can be broken into the right size for the fireplace, or if you know how to cut your own wood, split softwood such as pine into strips.

A few minutes before starting a fire, open the damper to allow the smoke to go up the chimney. Sometimes when a fire first begins, smoke comes back into the room because the chimney is not yet drawing the proper balance between inside and outside air. Next, take a rolled section of newspaper, light one end and hold it directly under the flue to prewarm the walls and start the draw. If there is still smoke, the house may be too airtight, so it may be necessary to crack a window until the fire gets going. Even the best fireplace can get backup puffs on windy days, but if this is a constant problem you might want to add a chimney cap. Also, eliminate any nearby tree that has grown tall enough to block airflow across the chimney, causing backpuffs down the flue. If these measures fail, the chimney may have serious problems that require professional help. To prepare for the fire, pile the kindling on top of rolled or crumpled newspaper placed toward the back of the fireplace between the andirons. Add two to three pieces of dry hardwood on top, then light the paper. As the fire gets going, use a poker to keep enough space between the logs so there is air for efficient burning. Once the fire has died out and is no longer smoldering, close the damper.

This will stop the warm air in the room from escaping up the chimney, and you will not be paying for fuel to heat the outside. Plan ahead to let the fire burn down completely before you go to bed; otherwise, if you close the damper too soon, the house will fill with smoke.

Ash Disposal

There are many sad stories about farmhouses that have burned to the ground because ashes were removed from a stove or fireplace, emptied into a paper bag or other flammable container, and then set on the porch. Be sure to put ashes into a metal container with a cover and let them sit outside on the ground until they are completely dead. Only then should ashes be transferred to a bag or trash can to save for use in the garden. Also, remember to keep combustibles like curtains, clothes, or furniture a minimum of three feet away from the woodstove, and have a fire extinguisher handy.

Just as in fireplaces, burning wood in stoves causes creosote buildup in the chimney. If it is not removed regularly, sparks can start a fire. With occasional use, the chimney will probably need to be cleaned once a year. However, if you burn the stove every day, the chimney may require cleaning as often as every six months. Frequent creosote buildup may indicate the stove is operating at too slow a burn rate.

Opposite:
A fireside scene as described by Mary Livermore on page 76, where "We could play, shout, run, jump, stand on the substantial chairs to look out the windows, play housekeeping, and set out the kitchen table with our little pewter dishes and tiny porringers, bring in our individual chairs, stools, and crickets, and build up establishments in every corner . . ."

Firewood

After you have made sure that all chimneys, fireplaces, or woodstoves are in proper working condition, it is time to build a woodpile of seasoned hardwood. "Seasoned" wood has been dried from four to twelve months. "Hardwood" refers to heavy wood that provides a long burn and gives out steady heat. It will not cause creosote to build up as quickly, and it will generally smoke and spark less than softwood. The hardwoods with the highest BTU ratings are shagbark hickory, black locust, white ash, red and white oak, beech, yellow birch, sugar maple, and cherry. Adding a few pieces of fragrant wood, like apple and cherry, is especially lovely.

You can obtain this wood by contacting local suppliers, or by cutting fallen and dying trees on your own property if you know how to cut wood. Once you know your area, you can scout other sources for wood to buy cheaply or get free: local orchards, town landfills, or private owners who want their land cleaned up. Wood is usually sold by the cord or by the "face" cord. Most people buy a face cord, a stack measuring four feet by eight feet with logs, or split wood, measuring one to two feet long. Wood is also sold by the truckload, with a standard half-ton pickup holding roughly one-third of a cord of wood. If you buy from your supplier in the spring, you will get the best price and have dry, seasoned wood for use in the late fall and winter. If you wait until the fall, the price will be higher. It's economical and great exercise to stack the wood yourself. Just make sure the wood is left close to your shed or stacking site. The first time you use a supplier, be present for the delivery to see that you receive the correct amount and that the wood is indeed seasoned (look at the cut ends; dry wood will have cracks). If you specified mixed hardwoods, don't accept any pine, cedar, or other softwood. Newly cut wood or green wood is always cheaper, but you will have to plan ahead. Delivered in the spring, it should be ready for use during the second winter.

If you live in the snowbelt, place the woodpile near your house so that it is easy to reach in the middle of winter. However, never place it directly against the house or inside, especially in the cellar, because bugs from the logs will invade wood siding or supporting beams. Much well-seasoned wood is likely to have been dead when it was cut, and is often home to the bugs that killed it. Make a platform for the pile to rest on from bricks, or wood pallets, and then stack the wood. The stack can be stabilized by placing at least one end against a tree or fence. If you buy green wood, stack it in a crisscross pattern to allow air to circulate, and place it where there is sun for at least part of the day. In the fall, cover it with a tarp to protect it from snow, ice, and rain. Flat-bottomed children's plastic sleds are an easy way to pull wood to the house across snow and mud.

Fireplace safety

Gertrude Lefferts Vanderbilt, writing in 1880 about the manners and customs of Dutch settlers, gives us a straightforward account of chimney cleaning that today would seem a risky practice:

A very rainy day, on which there was little or no wind, was taken advantage of as most suitable for the occasion. A huge bundle of straw tied on a pole was brought in from the barn, the fire in the fireplace was allowed to go out, and then this fagot of straw was lighted and held up the chimney. One man was stationed outside to watch if the rain extinguished every floating particle of straw or soot, for sometimes the flame reached beyond the chimney top; the roaring was like distant thunder, and, when the pole was withdrawn, a shower of fiery flakes and smutty tips of burning straw followed, like a dull, red shower, in the fireplace. There have not been many chimneys swept in that way in this town for the last thirty years, and yet it was at one time the only method of getting the chimneys clean. While upon the subject of chimneys and fires, we must digress to say that, during the last century, and even during the early part of the present, in case of the destruction of a house or barn by fire, or in any accident which occasioned pecuniary trouble, the neighbors and friends always came forward to assist in making up the loss. These pleasant, helpful acts certainly showed kind feeling between friends and neighbors, for there were no insurance offices and no fire alarms then; they depended upon each other.

Today being sure a fireplace is in good condition is extremely important for safety. New owners of farmhouses should check, when they move in and regularly afterward, that the mortar on the chimney is not crumbling, the flue has not cracked, and the firebricks are not loose or crumbling. Any of these conditions should be repaired as soon as possible. If the fireplace is used regularly, it is equally important to have the chimney cleaned every year, because creosote will accumulate in the flue, and sparks shooting upward can start a fire. Farmers have been known to remove creosote by pulling a small evergreen tree upside down through the chimney. This is not a recommended method. Most people call in chimney sweeps, who will also point out any problems found during cleaning. My chimney sweep advised me that there was a buildup of creosote in our chimney as a result of too many slow-burning fires. The way to minimize creosote, he said, is to have frequent hot, intense-burning fires. Smoldering overnight fires are a bad idea.

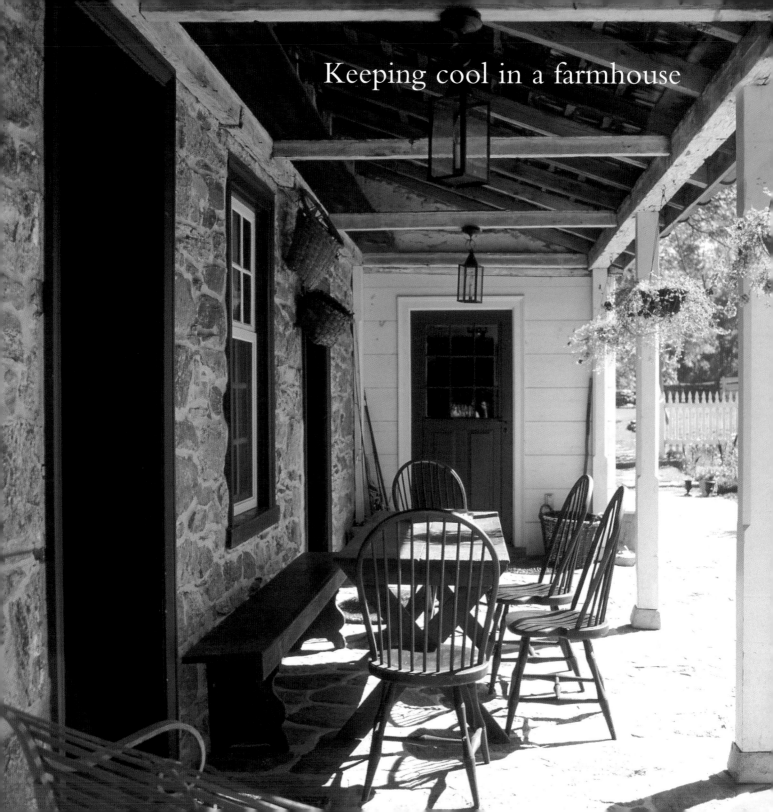

Keeping cool in a farmhouse

The gable-end view of this neat 1858 Illinois cobblestone farmhouse shows its semi-detached matching kitchen ell and small porch.

A familiar sound of summer in the country today is the squeak and slam of a screen door; they were new sounds in the nineteenth century though, indicating fresh air and freedom from flying insects. Previously, farmhouses that had been situated to offer the best protection and benefits from the elements could not be kept cool during the hottest months; the only recourse of inhabitants was to close the blinds and shutters or to plant shade trees. Stone-floored pantries and butteries, although often near the hot kitchen, were the coolest places. Summertime meant an invasion of flies as well as mosquitoes. Farmhouses also had nearby stables, barns, and piggeries, which attracted crawling and flying insects that then made their way into the house. Cheesecloth, or gauze covered with onion essence, had little effect on the onslaught.

In 1861 the Civil War broke out. As a result, a northern company's southern metal sieve business was shut down. This left a large amount of woven wire on hand, but an inventive employee soon changed that when he decided to give the sieve wire a coat of protective paint and offered it for sale as a door or window screen. It proved to be a vast improvement over the materials that had previously been used for this purpose. The metal screen industry was born.

South and west of New England the separate or summer kitchen appeared; sometimes a covered breezeway connected it to the main house. This reconstituted building may have been a farm's original log house, which was later overshadowed by a larger timber-framed or stone or brick home.

"Verandas are most desirable on the south and west sides of a house, for while they ward off the midday heat of summer, they still freely admit the low down winter sun."

E. H. Leyland, Farmhouses, 1882

In a study of the family farm in Pennsylvania, Amos Long Jr. saw the sense of the summer kitchen:

Although the structure was used for many functions, the preparation of food became the most important. Since most of the food for winter consumption was preserved during the summer months when the yields from the family garden and orchard were harvested and the cooking and eating were done here during the summer to eliminate the heat from the kitchen in the big house, the structure became known as the summer kitchen. The function of the summerhouse was geared to the needs of the farm family. It provided an excellent place to perform the many rougher household chores. In addition to eliminating fire, heat, flies and odors from the big kitchen, the separate summerhouse frequently avoided much confusion and disorder, it provided for better ventilation, and in its garret convenient accommodations for the "farm hands" or maid. From sometime in early spring until late fall, usually from April to October, depending on the weather, the various daily activities of the household from dawn until dusk were performed here. In this one room, with the aid of the fireplace, cook stove, or kitchen range, for heating and cooking, all the meals were prepared and served.

A separate kitchen in the South. The main house is seen through the window.

Opposite page: The back porch of a split-log Wisconsin farmhouse.

The farmhouse porch or veranda added as a lean-to came into North America from Africa, via the West Indian colonies. It had been relatively unknown in the mid-1700s, but by 1830 the porch was immensely popular as an addition that made the long day bearable. It became a shelter from the sun, and somewhere to keep firewood dry; most importantly, it was a living space between outside and inside—a long, cool room where one could work or rock on a chair when it was raining and watch the light change in the evening.

When porches were added to existing structures, they were often built upon inadequate or nonexistent foundations creating a history of problems, as the porch literally came apart from the farmhouse facade and sank to the ground, hastened by rot and hungry insects. Sadly, this has resulted in many porches being removed in the age of air-conditioning, and as we see new homes going up in the countryside it's rare to see a porch as part of the design. With farmhouses, especially with new owners, porches are valuable and should be maintained. New foundations or footings are much easier to install than in the past, though author James Howard Kunstler insists that porches less than six feet deep are useless, because there is not enough room to sit down and look out, let alone move around. With a proper porch or veranda, a simple idea creates an out-looking social feeling in rural communities.

A look into a historic twenty-eight-foot-square Louisiana house from its generous overhanging gallery.

Opposite: *The white porch of a Victorian farmhouse in Chaska, Minnesota, that now operates as a bed-and-breakfast inn (see page 195).*

Tasks

Farmhouse tasks were carried out by women and children until the boys were old enough to work on the land. Just as important and almost as numerous were jobs in the farmyard, vegetable garden, and the buildings nearby, which were supervised by the farmer's wife. In the house, apart from the creative tasks like baking and needlework, most chores were onerous, achingly repetitive, and physically taxing.

Sally McMurry, the author of *Families and Farmhouses in Nineteenth-Century America,* found this poem in an 1876 issue of the *Prairie Farmer:*

Work, work, work,
Is ever the farmer's song,
There's never a time to stop and think
Be the evenings ever so long.

Yes work, work, work
Till your hands are hard and rough;
Work, and wring, and scrape,
Till your finger nails wear off.

And then sit down and write
Of the joys of a farmer's life;
'Tis, oh, to be a slave,
Or a modern farmer's wife.

Oh no, the men are not to blame,
For they do all they can;
But then there are a hundred things
That are beyond a man.

They do their work, then go to sleep.
No "yeast," is on their minds;
If all the babies wake and weep,
It ne'er disturbs a man.

It's work, work, work,
Yes, cook, and weed, and hoe,
Till our ladylike and dimpled hands
Are not as white as snow.

I would that I were dead,
And buried in a row,
Under a fragrant cabbage head,
And at my feet a hoe.

But I can't die, I have no time,
'Twould take a day or two,
And stop the plow,
So I must wait
'Till the busy time is through.

Far left:
The plain kitchen of a historic Finnish settler's farm in Wisconsin. The two labor-saving devices, an early rocking washing machine in the foreground and a barrel butter churn just beyond it, were extremely hard to operate, requiring strong arms, wrists, and willpower.

Left:
A modern appliance is somewhat disguised in the kitchen of an Ohio log home.

Here are three separate working days as seen through the eyes of young girls:

When I was about ten a woman, who lived about a mile from us, came to see Mother. She wanted her to let me go and keep house for her for a week. She had two little girls and her aged Father to leive [leave] in my care. Mother let me go and told me to work like a little spider. The first morning the old man called me at five o'clock to get up and get his breakfast. I got up and went to the well after a pail of water; it was quite a distance from the house that I had to carry the water. Then I boiled some potatoes and fried pork and made coffee. I had to cook over a fire place, hang[ing] the kittles on hooks that were hung on a crane that would swing off the fire when the things were cooked. I set the coffee pot on some coals on the hearth. After I had cleered [sic] away, I put on some beans to stew for dinner and had enough left over to last two or three days. Then I made some buiscuit [sic] and baked them in a tin baker, set before the fire. The little girls went to school every day and I was alone, for the old Man slept most of the time. One day there came up a most terrific thunder shower and frightened me half to death, but the old Man slipted [slept] through it all. The woman came home at the end of a week and gave me a nine-pence for my weeks [sic] work, and I bought me a new calico apron . . .
—From *Childish Things, The Reminiscence of Susan Baker Blunt*

In 1879, a ninety-year-old Sarah Smith Emery published the following account of her youth in *Reminiscences of a Nonagenerian:*

In those summer days, when my recollection first opens, mother and Aunt Sarah rose in the early dawn, and, taking the well-scoured wooden pails from the bench by the back door, repaired to the cow yard behind the barn. We owned six cows; my grandmother four. Having milked the ten cows, the milk was strained, the fires built, and breakfast prepared. Many families had milk for this meal, but we always had coffee or chocolate, with meat and potatoes.

During breakfast the milk for the cheese was warming over the fire, in the large brass kettle . . . The curd having been broken into the basket, the dishes were washed, and unless there was washing or other extra work, the house was righted. By the time this was done the curd was ready for the [cheese] press.

Next came preparations for dinner, which was on the table punctually at twelve o'clock. In the hot weather we usually had boiled salted meat and vegetables, and, if it was baking day, a custard or pudding. If there was linen whitening on the grass, as was usual at this season, that must be sprinkled. After dinner the cheeses were turned and rubbed; then mother put on a clean frock, and dressed herself for the afternoon. Our gowns and aprons, unless upon some special occasion, when calico was worn, were usually of blue-checked homemade gingham, starched and ironed to a nice gloss.

In the sultry August afternoons mother and Aunt Sarah usually took their sewing to the cool back room, whose shaded door and windows overlooked the freshly mown field, dotted by apple trees . . . At five o'clock the men came from the field, and tea was served. The tea things were washed, the vegetables were gathered for the morrow, the linen taken in, and other chores done. At sunset the cows came from the pasture. Milking finished and the milk strained, the day's labor was ended. The last load pitched on the hay mow . . . my father and the hired man joined us in the cool back room, where bowls of bread and milk were ready for those who wished the refreshment. At nine o'clock the house was still, the tired hands gladly resting from the day's toil.

What appears to be a corner of a cool pantry is, in fact, the inside of a large inglenook fireplace at the end of the stone-built Barnes-Brinton House in Chadds Ford, Pennsylvania. It was not uncommon in German-American homes to have such a window built into the fireplace. With so much work going on there, the natural light was a valuable asset.

The following is an account from *Oldtown Folks* by Harriet Beecher Stowe, published in 1869:

Our daily life began at four o'clock in the morning, when the tapping of Aunt Lois's imperative heels on the back stairs, and her authoritative rap at our door, dispelled my slumbers . . . It imposed in the first place the necessity of my quitting my warm bed in a room where the thermometer must have stood below zero, and where the snow, drifting through the loosely framed window, often lay in long wreaths on the floor.

As Aunt Lois always opened the door and set in a lighted candle, one of my sinful amusements consisted in lying and admiring the forest of glittering frost-work which had been made by our breath freezing upon the threads of the blanket. I sometimes saw rainbow colors in this frost-work, and went off into dreams and fancies about it, which ended in a doze, from which I was awakened, perhaps, by some of the snow from the floor rubbed smartly on my face, and the words, "How many times must you be called?" and opened my eyes to the vision of Aunt Lois standing over me indignant and admonitory.

Then I would wake Harry. We would spring from the bed and hurry on our clothes, buttoning them with fingers numb with cold, and run down to the back sink-room, where, in water that flew off in icy spatters, we performed our morning ablutions, refreshing our faces and hands by a brisk rub upon a coarse rolling-towel of brown homespun linen. Then with mittens, hats, and comforters, we were ready to turn out with old Caesar [an African-American hired man] to the barn to help him fodder the cattle . . .

Then came the feeding of the hens and chickens and other poultry, a work in which we especially delighted, going altogether beyond Caesar in our largesses of corn . . . In very severe weather we sometimes found hens or turkeys so overcome with the cold as to require, in Caesar's view, hospital treatment . . .

My grandmother bestirred herself promptly, compounding messes of Indian-meal enlivened with peppercorns, which were forced . . . down the long throat, and which in due time acted as a restorative . . .

A natural, and apparently inexhaustible, material for making candles was found in all the colonies in the waxy fruit borne by the bayberry bush. In 1748 a Swedish naturalist, visiting America, wrote an account of the bayberry wax:

There is a plant here from the berries of which they make a kind of wax or tallow, and for that reason the Swedes call it the tallow-shrub. The English call the same tree the candle-berry tree or bayberry bush; it grows abundantly in a wet soil, and seems to thrive particularly well in the neighborhood of the sea. The berries look as if flour had been strewed on them. They are gathered late in Autumn, being ripe about that time, and are thrown into a kettle or pot full of boiling water; by this means their fat melts out, floats at the top of the water, and may be skimmed off into a vessel; with the skimming they go on till there is no tallow left. The tallow, as soon as it is congealed, looks like common tallow or wax, but has a dirty green color. By being melted over and refined it acquires a fine and transparent green color. This tallow is dearer than common tallow, but cheaper than wax. Candles of this size do not easily bend, nor melt in summer as common candles do; they burn better and slower, nor do they cause any smoke, but yield rather an agreeable smell when they are extinguished. In Carolina they not only make candles out of the wax of the berries, but likewise sealing-wax.

Robert Beverley a historian of Virginia in 1705, wrote of the smell of burning bayberry tallow: "If an accident puts a candle out, it yields a pleasant fragrancy to all that are in the room; insomuch that nice people often put them out on purpose to have the incense of the expiring snuff."

Bayberries were of enough importance to have some laws made to protect them. Everywhere on Long Island grew the stunted bushes, and everywhere they were valued. In 1687, the town of Brookhaven forbade the gathering of the berries before September 15, under penalty of a fine of fifteen shillings.

Candles burn on a cold morning in the children's chamber of the Sheldon-Hawkes House in Deerfield, Massachusetts. Under the window, the furniture includes a small slant-front desk and a child's banister-back chair.

The interior of a German kitchen at the historic Koepsell farm in Wisconsin (see page 53). The stove had to be fed continually with wood and needed to be emptied of its ashes twice a day. Iron stoves were difficult to get used to. The farmwife had to overcome its intricacies and implements, and keep it clean with blacking. No two early stoves behaved quite the same.

Bread and water

The Pennsylvania German Society published a photographic essay accurately recording the routines of farmwork in the early twentieth century. Accompanying an image of a woman using a traditional bake oven was this caption:

The various days of a woman's week were assigned specific chores. This was so strong a pattern that a popular song in the dialect celebrated these activities. Friday was universally baking day. Thursday evening the bread dough was set to rise. Early Friday the oven was heated by building a fire in its cavern which would be raked out once the walls had reached the desired temperature. Meanwhile the bread dough was divided into the rye straw bread baskets . . . to rise again. Other cakes and pies were prepared. The bread was baked at the back of the oven because it remained in the oven longest, the fruit pies with lids in the center and the custards and tarts in the front. These had to last a week so that the quantity was substantial. Since Good Friday always fell on baking day, but was a day for no labor, no baking was done then. "Don't even look into the oven on Good Friday, for you are looking into a grave."

Mary Livermore remembered in her 1899 autobiography, *The Story of My Life*, that

The well-laid-out storage room off of the kitchen of a restored nineteenth-century Ohio farmhouse, with easily accessible yellowware.

she frequently needed to ask her minister husband for advice on domestic matters; he had been fortunate to come from a farming family:

We had a small brick oven in our hired house, and remembering how easily my mother had managed a larger one, and how much she had accomplished with it, I resolved to make use of the more convenient one at my service, and, one day, heated it. After the bed of glowing coals had been removed from the oven, it remained intensely hot, and I had no idea at what temperature it should be used. So, thermometer in hand, I mounted the stairs to my husband's study, and laid my "newest grief" before him. He had become used to listening to my perplexities, and accustomed to my interruptions.

"Do you know at what degree the thermometer must stand in a brick oven, when it is hot enough for baking?"

"Oh, we never used thermometers to gauge the heat of an oven when I was a boy; my mother would hold her hand in the oven till she could count twenty. When she could do that, the oven was at the right heat."

By and by, I ran across another problem. Another ascent of the stairs—another invasion of my poor husband's premises—another question from the domestic catechism.

"Excuse me for coming again, but, really, I don't seem to know anything. I'm baking cake and you know half the time it doesn't get done in the middle. Can you tell me how a person can be sure that a loaf of cake is baked through?"

"This was my mother's test. She ran a broom straw through the middle of the cake. If it came out clean the cake was done. But if it was moist and sticky, it needed more baking. I have tried cake for her with a broom straw many a time."

Vegetables being prepared on the kitchen table of a home in Yorkville, Illinois.

Operating a pump was hard work and it had to be done several times a day; then the water had to be carried into the farmhouse. In 1886, a calculation was made that a typical North Carolina farmwife would have to bring water from a pump, well, or spring, eight to ten times each day. A load of washing needed about fifty gallons of water. It worked out that she covered 148 miles and carried over 36 tons of water in the course of one year.

Doing the laundry in the days before washers and dryers was a miserable chore and the white of Monday's wash did not improve the black mood of the women of the farmhouse. The men and boys made themselves scarce and were prepared for cold dinners and hot tempers when they came in. The good thing was that clean clothing was always welcome on a busy farm and in the spring and summer country folk had an advantage over their city friends, as anyone who has worn garments aired and dried by the wind and sun on a clothesline can attest.

Where life was numbingly rote, tasks gave sense of purpose to a woman living in a sod house in Nebraska writing to her husband. "I will tell you what I was doing most of last week I tore up a lot of rags and knit a Rug it will be about 1 yd square when finished I could have finished it yesterday had I worked at it I knit it in strips and then sewed them together knit them on wooden Needles I dont think I will ever knit another as it is hard work and they are not so nice as braided ones."

Sir Anthony Fitzherbert in his 1552 treatise on husbandry said, "It is the duty of the wife to winnow all manner of corn [wheat], to make malt, to wash and to wring, to make hay, to shear corn, and in time of need to help her husband fill the muckwains or dung cart; to drive the plough, to load corn, hay and such other, and to go on a ride to market; to sell butter, cheese, milk, eggs, chickens, capons, hens, pigs, geese and all manner of corn." She then could take the rest of the day off.

Pickling

The great art in making good pickles is to have good vinegar. The best vinegar for pickling is made of sound cider. As good vinegar is not always at hand, the best way is to prepare a brine strong enough to bear an egg. When the tub is full of pickles, allow the brine to cover them; then cover them over with cabbage-leaves, and a board and weight to keep them in the brine. For use, freshen in warm water, and put them in a bright brass kettle, with vinegar enough to cover them, and scald them 15 or 20 minutes; put them in jars, and pour hot vinegar over them; flavor them with cloves, mace, black pepper, an onion or two, and a little horseradish and ginger.

—*Facts for Farmers,* 1866

Above: *The pantry of a historic farmhouse in Michigan. The traylike object on the bottom shelf is a butter worker, used to remove buttermilk from newly churned butter. On the shelf above is a cutter for slicing cabbage into sauerkraut.*
Right: *The kitchen of a historic German farmhouse in Wisconsin. The water for washing clothes was heated in the large pot hanging on the wall.*

Cellars

Farmhouse cellars, the very necessary underground household stores, were not common in the old world. The civilized settlers, making their first earth-fast, wood-lined shelters, knew only of cellars in the grander houses of England, but as they urgently dug down into the ground to survive the first winter, they started a cellar tradition when building homes that continued into the twentieth century. Realizing that they were in a climate more extreme than that in Northern Europe, an underground store would keep their food fit to eat in a cool, dry place when the weather was hot or freezing. The cellar did not always extend under the whole ground floor but was usually under the main part of the farmhouse, giving some extra insulation to rooms above it. It was descended to by a steep stairway.

Few old farmhouses had a cellar foundation under the entire structure. Early cellar foundations were constructed with large, flat native stones. Later foundations were constructed of field stones with the gaps filled with mortar. Remarkably, many old foundations are still firmly in place. Before the use of concrete (farmers were suspicious of anything that would crack) cellars had clay floors, some with flat stones or bricks laid to provide a walkway. At the coming of winter, the outsides were banked with earth, and near any potential opening in the cellar foundation, corn stalks, straw, or leaves were piled to help protect against the wind and cold and to keep snakes, and mice, rats, and other rodents outside.

The following is an early account of a cellar's contents:

. . . stoneware jars (with rocks placed on the lids to keep them closed) might be filled with pickles, molasses, apple butter and pickled meats. Carrots were packed in moist sand in the basement, and potatoes were buried under straw. The cellar was used to store butter and cheese, as well as eggs. Since animal fat was important—used for making soap, candles and shortening—after butchering cellars were often piled with stands of lard. Mass-produced glass jars available in the early 1920s were much cheaper than hand-blown jars, and these, along with pressure cookers in the 1930s, led to wide-spread home canning. Industrious women filled their cellar shelves with jars of green beans, tomatoes, fruits, peas, corn, relishes and pickles.

The farmhouse cellar today usually houses the heating machinery, a spare refrigerator, and washer and dryer, making it too warm and crowded to do anything that it was originally intended for, although a dark corner or crawl space can be useful as storage.

In 1880, Gertrude Lefferts Vanderbilt recalled:

The cellars were carefully built, with a view to being cool in summer and warm in winter; to accomplish this they were of rough, unhewn stone, with brick or earthen floors. To insure perfect cleanliness, the neat housewife had them thoroughly whitewashed semiannually; but, in spite of all her efforts, there was sometimes an unpleasant odor coming up from the great heaps of potatoes, turnips, and parsnips. This was especially the case toward spring, when the farmer set his men at work turning the potato heaps and pulling off the sprouts which the warmth of the cellar may have caused to grow. This sometimes was occasioned by the want of ventilation in the cellars, for it was customary in the autumn to close up the windows and gratings with salt bay, which was tightly packed against every opening, leaving only toward the southern exposure some entrance for a gleam of sunshine. A candle, or the open cellar-door, gave the visitor to these apartments the only means of picking his way there from December to March.

The furnaces with which we heat our dwellings would render such storage of winter provisions at the present time impossible, even were there not other reasons which make such a course unnecessary.

Here in these cellars might be seen huge hogsheads of salted beef, barrels of salted pork, hams in brine before they were smoked, firkins of salted shad and mackerel, firkins of home-made butter and lard, stone jars of pickles, and little kegs of pigs' feet in vinegar, called souse.

Festoons of sausage hung in the cold-cellar pantry, "rolliches" and head-cheese were on the swinging shelf, which was constructed as a protection against the foraging mice.

In another portion of the cellar were bins for the potatoes, turnips, and parsnips. There were great heaps of apples for cooking or common use, barrels of apples of more choice varieties; barrels of vinegar, and of cider, and at the foundation of the kitchen chimney there was a receptacle for wood-ashes from the fireplaces above, to be used for lye in the making of soap.

Thus the cellar in the homestead was the great storage place for the provisions of nearly the entire year.

This Minnesota farm-house root cellar was a modern convenience when the house was built: it was directly accessible from the kitchen by inside stairs, saving the family and hired help an outside trip in the winter. The door at the left leads to a cold storage space for dairy products, which was another convenience, since most people had to walk to their spring-houses to fetch butter, cheese, and milk. The room was whitewashed yearly to brighten and disinfect it.

Today, the cellar stores the historic varieties of root vegetables the farm raises. The bins hold potatoes and rutabagas between layers of earth. In the nineteenth century, the pumpkins would have been grown as food for livestock.

Other spaces and storage

Farmhouse attics and garrets were used in a number of ways and some were insulated with sawdust. They were used as sleeping quarters for members of the family and the help; in the early days, they were fitted with bins to store grain, and to hang and dry fruit, vegetables, and smoked meat. Spinning wheels for flax and wool ended up there as the availability of cotton made them less necessary downstairs. And as Gertrude Lefferts Vanderbilt wrote:

It was in this roomy garret that the careful housewife had the week's washing hung in stormy weather; the clothes-lines were stretched from side to side, and thus, when in winter the ground was covered with snow, it was a convenience to have the great basket of wet clothes carried up and hung out here, to freeze and dry undisturbed and out of the way; for in those days the laundry was not a room apart, the washing and ironing being done in the kitchen.

Sheared wool is conditioned under the eaves at a restored log farmhouse located in Sullivan, Wisconsin.

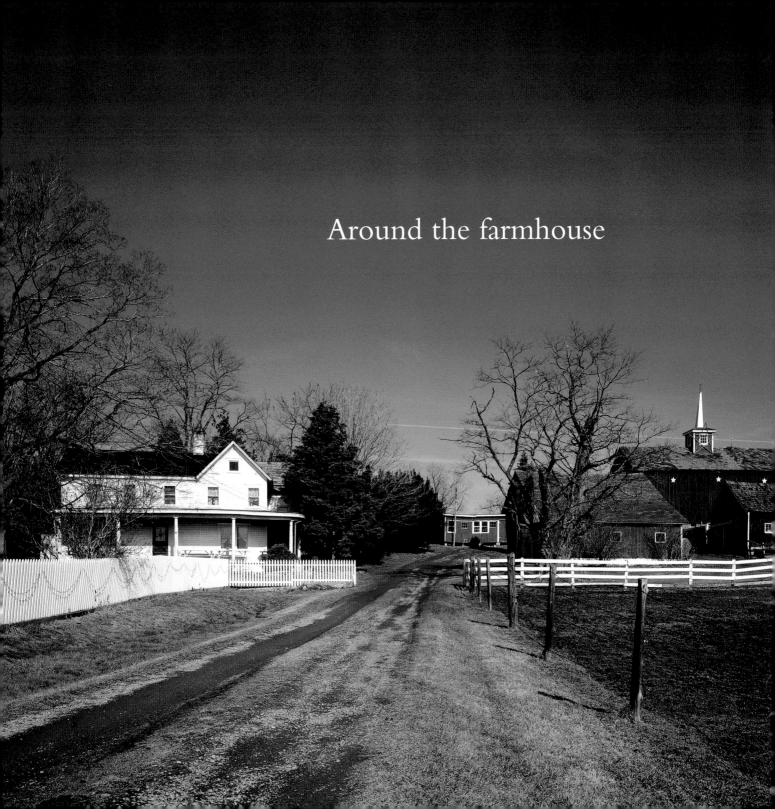

Around the farmhouse

Immigrants who came to America from Europe remembered farmyards with buildings set around a muddy square, or in a row, one against the wall of the next. In America, the availability of space and timber often resulted in collections of structures that appeared—to the European eye—to have been dropped gently from space. This arrangement bespeaks a kind of confidence, a sense of independence, and an openness, as if to say, "We don't care what we look like." The only boundaries might be a picket fence around the farm's vegetable garden and orchard, or perhaps a fenced stock pen. In many of today's suburbs, deliberately repetitive landscaping and identical front lawns give the impression of a conforming society. A cluster of American farm buildings has the opposite effect—it exhibits a very real sense of freedom in its disposition.

At first the farmyard layout may seem indiscriminate. It is difficult to know the order in which buildings were constructed and why they were placed where they were, until an understanding of the strategy emerges. The barn, for example, is likely to have been placed farthest away from the farmhouse—to keep it away from the dangerous sparks of the house chimney. The first farms were designed along the trail connecting them to the next settlement, so the entrances faced on the road on both sides.

An old barn would have its big doors facing the prevailing wind to make threshing easier. If there was a slope, the farmer might use it to provide a barn foundation and to create space for cattle stalls so that hay and feed could be driven in and dropped down from the level above. The dairy would be near the house, but the smokehouse and privy were maintained at a respectable distance.

Sometimes it takes a bit of thought and experience to decide what a particular building was designed for. If there was no barn, at least there would be a structure that once served as a wagon shed, carriage house, or a stable, and ended up a garage-cum-woodshed. Nearly every farmhouse grew lean-to additions, or ells. In the Northeast, in Maine and New Hampshire, the linear habit of northern England took root again. Later, as farms became more organized, buildings including the main house, little house, privy, and barn were linked together for comfort and efficiency. In most parts of the country, however, buildings remained separate, even though in some cases they were connected by a dogtrot or other such device. As farming changed, buildings large and small were either left in place and used for other purposes or allowed to crumble. Nearly every old property has on it, along with the house, the foundation of another building of some kind.

Farm buildings in America can be roughly divided into two groups, vernacular and folk. The vernacular are workaday buildings around a farm likely dating from the mid-nineteenth century and following plans obtained by suppliers, or constructed by local builders with one tried-and-true style—commonplace, but well built and designed. These buildings illustrated the farm's growth and established its size or even its decline. Most standing stables, carriage houses, cribs, sheds, barns, and other outbuildings don't reveal the history, roots, or culture of the particular farm family who built the house. The other group is what has been called

A white farmyard gate contrasts with the workaday split-rail fencing and logs of this historic plantation in Georgia.

folk architecture. This is truly local, using local materials and often built by the first farmers themselves with no plans, just the firmly implanted traditions and styles of the old country.

Whether vernacular or folk, the working structures on a farm needed a lot more ventilation than did the house: the hay barracks, corncribs, and barns to keep the contents dry; the springhouse to keep the water cool; and the dairy to keep the milk and cream from spoiling. The stables, piggeries, and chicken coops needed fresh air for the health of the animals. These requirements meant that the buildings were very cold in the winter. Today they frustrate many who want to use such buildings for living and work, since their infrastructure makes insulating them difficult and expensive.

When old farmhouses were built on rock shelves, root crops were stored in a separate cellar, usually located in a slope nearby. These were mostly made of stone, with three sides built into the hill and the fourth side facing south. They were long as well as deep, with the contents held in place by the walls and separated by boards. Other root cellars were built as mounds on flatter ground, with steps leading down to the door. Anything stored was always below the frost line.

In heavily wooded areas, settlers felled young trees and put up log fences. When the first timber-framed houses were built in new clearings, the trunks of young, straight trees were laid one on top of another to make simple fences. They went up in no time, their stability improved by occasional chocks. In time, thrifty farmers noticed that they could use half as much wood if they split the logs. This was the beginning of the rail fence. Up in the hills, rocks were either piled in the angle or against the rails. Evidence of this can still be found where the rails have long gone but signs of a wall remain. "Snake" fences were built with pride, but they took up a lot of land. At every turn in their crux a rail called a rider was laid. It was hard to knock down.

A "snake" fence meets a stone wall at the historic Rebecca Nurse Homestead in Danvers, Massachusetts.

A cutting garden within a picket fence in Rochester, Minnesota.

Recycled wooden-framed window sashes form the cover of a cold-frame at a historic nineteenth-century farm in Minnesota. They serve to prolong the growing season in northern Minnesota. Here, they protect a late crop of fall greens, including turnip greens, lettuce, and beet greens. The pine-board fence, surrounding just the kitchen garden, protects the vegetables from foraging domestic animals, such as young pigs and chickens.

A privy is seen at the edge of an aromatic herb garden near an 1858 midwestern farmhouse.

Conveniently near the kitchen door, the vegetable garden was like a farm in miniature. The plot had to be plowed or dug, fertilized, weeded, and harvested in the same farming year. The farmhouse gardens were always in the most convenient spot. Today, though, aesthetics have become increasingly important. New arrivals to the country have often moved the garden patch farther away from the home, preferring a flower-edged lawn, and have paid the price. Tucking a garden away from sight, even when fenced, invites unwelcome visitors. The farmwife put her plot in the middle of an open area. This was usually effective enough to keep unwanted visitors away, and there was no need for fencing. Rodents, deer, and birds prefer cover—to come from or run to when discovered—and avoid open spots instinctively. An open plan made digging, tilling, and altering the size of the garden much easier, as well.

Farmwives loved their flowers too. In his 1885 history of the area, Henry B. Plumb writes of the farmhouses of the Wyoming Valley in Pennsylvania circa 1790:

In these early times the people, though surrounded with stumps and stones and brush and woods and the general disorder of new clearings, had some taste for the beautiful. Every house had a clump of rose bushes in the door-yard or in the garden and a bunch or two of peonies, a clump of lilac bushes, sunflowers and hollyhocks . . . If there were young girls in the family they would have pinks, pansies, marigolds, and morning glories and as many other kinds of flowers as they could get.

Opposite:
A farmhouse flower garden in Rochester, Minnesota, seen at its best in high summer.

House stories

A moved building is preferable to a destroyed one. Although some farmhouses, barns, and outbuildings may be redundant on the landscape, they retain their simple dignity. When a building is in danger and can be removed from its original site, the structure is photographed, measured and drawn, disassembled, and moved. As it is disassembled, the value of the building becomes more apparent. The layers of construction are removed, revealing parts of older buildings, fragments of original paint or wallpaper, and ephemeral traces of the people who lived there before, such as inscriptions behind plastered walls and woodwork and newspapers stuffed between floorboards for insulation.

What follows are some examples of how historic American farmhouse buildings have been restored and, in some cases, moved. On their original and new sites, great care is paid to their accurate restoration and rebuilding, giving them the attention they need to remain living buildings for generations to come. Here too, are some, mostly faithful, copies in the Midwest, where the owners' enthusiasm for all things historically New England has held sway over the local vernacular models. The rooms sometimes contain an excess of stoneware crocks and "stuff" that is collected rather than used. But the houses are interesting because of what they describe on the landscape, more than for what their interiors say about an imagined past.

The Burroughs House in western New Jersey. An enlarged view is shown on the two previous pages.

The Burroughs House, had been abandoned about four or five years before it was relocated. A former resident of the house, who had thought that the building had been destroyed by fire, discovered that it was still standing but in jeopardy. He originally planned to move the structure to New England, but eventually another site was found, only a couple of miles from the original location. Although the house was moved from its original context, it has remained very much part of the local vernacular. The original clean lines of the Georgian-style main house survive, although the windows and their placement on the back of the house are not original.

The owner wanted to expand the house from about 3,000 square feet to about 5,000 square feet. The stone wing at right is a new addition, loosely based on historical precedent. The orientation of the original buildings was also changed, with the Dutch wing moved to the left of the main house to complement the new site. The shutters, the transom over the front door, and the cellar windows were not found on the original house, but all are based on historical and regional precedents.

The stone veneer on the new wing is ten inches thick, much thicker than most veneers. The stone came from digging the foundation for the house in its new location, from the house's original foundation, and from a farmhouse that used to be on this property. All of the colors and types are indigenous to this property and region. The biggest stones are quoin stones, which define the corners. Between them, there are many horizontal stones, with a few larger ones mixed in, which is typical of early houses. In later years, when quarrying became widespread, larger stones were used throughout.

The parlor in the main section of the house was restored to its original layout, with a closet to the left of the fireplace where an exterior door had been added. One of the carpenters on the project made new dog-eared architraves to match those surviving above the cupboard. As was often the case in well-kept farmhouses, the fireplace brick was not meant to he exposed and was covered with a coat of mortar and whitewash to reflect light into the room. The floorboards are not original, but are early yellow pine.

All the stones of the large cooking fireplace in the Dutch wing have been put back into their original locations and whitewashed, as was the practice when the building was a working kitchen. Around the early- to mid-nineteenth century, cookstoves and heating stoves replaced open fires and were inserted into the fireplace, as the owner has done here. The mantel shelf was constructed from evidence found in the walls of the original structure. The window next to the fireplace is also typical of working kitchens, bringing light into houses that were considerably darker than modern Americans are accustomed to.

The staircase to the right of the fireplace had been removed when the original house was found, but enough regional precedent existed to believe that it was constructed in this manner. The second-floor loft would have been used by farm laborers and was not directly connected to the main house. The floor joists are exposed, as they were in Dutch houses. At the far left is the Dutch door, part of which comes from an original Dutch door from another property.

This homestead in Chester County, Pennsylvania, has had a long and painstaking restoration. When the early-nineteenth-century, three-bay stone house was bought in 1976 it had no running water or electricity, but did have its original window sashes and floors. The new owners came home from their day jobs and ate by candlelight for a year until power was installed. The home was what they could afford and for twenty years they lived in two rooms, and a porch that had been converted to a kitchen, and raised a family. When the husband was excavating for an oil tank, he discovered the stone foundation of what turned out to have been a log house, dismantled when the new house was being erected. He found the corners of the gable end and chimney base, which gave him an approximation of the log house dimensions. By 1995 the couple had completed the restoration of the stone house and barns, and wanted to recreate the log house. They found an intact building in south-central Pennsylvania of the right dimensions, now re-erected over the original foundation, housing a new kitchen, and adjoining its stone partner.

In Suffield, Ohio, a couple have forged a connection to New England while restoring and adapting a local farmhouse built in 1870.

Looking as if the house beyond followed the fortunes of settlers starting out in a frontier cabin, the reverse is true; the log building in the photograph on the left is an addition. Although older than the 1870 farmhouse, it arrived from North Carolina in 1995.

The owners worked hard laying and chinking the 18-by-18-foot massive oak logs themselves, raising the roof, and laying floorboards. They hired a mason to build the chimney. The log addition serves as a keeping room and is linked to the main building by a small log buttery.

Everywhere in this Ohio living room and through to the dining room is evidence of the owners' enthusiasm for anything that has a connection to New England—the eighteenth-century chandelier that holds their homemade candles, the Connecticut long-case clock, and the New England pewterware and chests evoking a different time and place.

The attractive 1870 farmhouse.

In the foreground, resting on a one-board Ohio kitchen table, is an eighteenth-century New England maple bowl with its inevitable crack stabilized by twine. The neat shelf arrangement between the doors holds a small collection of Pennsylvania redware.

In 1993 a restored 1815 log farmhouse was destroyed by fire. It had been the home of an interior decorator of period houses, and everything in it was lost. Despite the devastation, the owner decided to rebuild on the spot and interestingly she took advantage of remodeling codes that allowed her to retain the lower ceiling heights of two hundred years before. The style of the structure follows the Richardson House in Old Sturbridge Village, Massachusetts.

The parlor has a barrel-back Deerfield corner cupboard with its original salmon-colored paint. On the bare wide-plank pine-board floor is a reminder that in early houses painted floorcloths were more common than carpets.

The keeping room in the rebuilt home. Behind arranged metal fireplace clutter is a mantel found at an auction in Canton, and to the right of the opening there is an oven door from Connecticut. The color scheme is influenced by that of the basement kitchen of the Salem House in Old Sturbridge Village.

Again, the influence of
Old Sturbridge Village
is seen in the guest
bedroom. The stencil-
patterned walls are
copied from the
Richardson House.
The washstand still has
its original paint and
decoration. The old
pencil-post bedstead has
a fishnet canopy.

The front of the Cape farmhouse.

There seems to be a strong attraction in the Midwest for a connection to New England farmhouses. In this section there are examples of new saltboxes in Illinois and Ohio, and here is a 1790's New Hampshire Cape farmhouse that fulfilled a need an Illinois woman had to find a two-hundred-year-old home somewhere in Yankee heartland. The farmhouse also serves as a base for her antique dealing, but more importantly, two or three historic skills are perpetuated here; hearth-cooked dinners for private parties, brick-oven baking, and the forming of historically accurate sugar loaves. Another skill is more decorative: she specializes in the Rufus Porter-style murals and faux finishes covering her walls, and completes commissions for other homeowners.

The open door shows the small front hall and its only decoration—a Rufus Porter-style mural.

The view from the
first-floor bedchamber
shows an eighteenth-
century cradle and the
back of an eighteenth-
century side chair.
The streaked, aged
effect is all over the
interior walls.

To the right of the
dining room fireplace is
an early-nineteenth-
century settle chair with
its original paint. The
bowl on the shelf above
is a hollowed-out gourd.
The blanket-warming
crane above the fireplace
was useful on cold New
England nights.

In the dining room a hand-embroidered cornice board runs across the window sashes. Its pattern complements that of the side chair next to the painted dresser. The old pine floorboards are about two feet wide.

The first-floor bedchamber was once used as a parlor.

Opposite page: A reproduction mouse perches near an old gnawed opening at the dresser drawers. On the shelf is a sugar loaf formed by the owner.

Although no barnhouses survived from the Dutch settlement areas in the Hudson Valley, one has emerged in Wisconsin. This 1894 "house-barn" was built by immigrants from Finland. It had a dividing wall that separated the domestic half from the livestock.

About to be demolished in a forest then scheduled to be clear-cut, the red pine log structure was dismantled and driven on two flat-bed trucks to a new ninety-three-acre site on a working farm in the southeastern part of the state. Today, the entire building is used as a home. Other rescued vintage farm structures shelter the animals. The couple raises several rare breeds of sheep including the Jacob; some of its wool is seen being aired on the loft floor on page 126.

Apart from the many activities at the farm, the husband restores log structures and is a landscape architect, and constructed the pond in the foreground to encourage wildlife.

A porch was added to the side of the house.

A rescued fachwerk building is seen in front of a log barn.

In the dining room a chandelier hangs from one of the original house-barn's rough-cut beams. Below it is an 1850 cherry refectory table.

The second-floor rooms take advantage of the original barn's vaulted ceiling, and a fine combination of simply hewn and finely carved wood is highlighted in the bedroom.

In 1848, Anson Davis raised a handsome and spacious brick house along the Hayden Run in Washington Township, Ohio. The brick for the house was fired at the kiln just across the road on a farm belonging to his brother-in-law. After the main block of the house was completed, work was immediately begun on a two-story kitchen wing at the back, which was completed in 1854.

In the large entry hall, a slightly curving stairway leads to the second floor. The rail and balusters are of cherry wood, and the wall is decorated by a Rufus Porter-style land-scape mural.

In the Anson Davis home, regional patterns emerge in the use of local materials such as the brick which was kiln-fired across the road; the walnut, American chestnut, and oak woods used in the mantels, doors, and windows; and the limestone found nearby for the window lintels and porch steps. These materials were used in a fairly simple state, and yet constructed with a refined craftsmanship reflected in the symmetry of proportion in their design. The stone, brick, and timber of the house convey a sense of weight and permanence.

The kitchen has been modernized with great care, achieving a simple, practical appearance, yet light-filled and inviting. The traditional soapstone sink is well placed under the window.

*Vintage linens and textiles are on the high-posted bed and in the cradle. On the far wall,
to the left of the door, is an antique armoire.*

In the keeping room, the wooden bench has a rail to safeguard a sleeping child. In the far corner is a screened food cupboard.

The stone-walled dining room.

For the last seventeen years of his life, Daniel Boone lived in this house. He built it with the help of his youngest son, Nathan, in 1803. The large home in Defiance, Missouri, has seven fireplaces and rises to four stories including a below-ground level that has a kitchen and a dining room. The limestone walls are two-and-a-half-feet thick.

Living history is an important activity at the homestead, with classes in which artisans teach rural skills such as weaving, lace making, canning, spinning, soap making, and open-hearth cooking. The homestead is open to visitors from mid-March to mid-December.

The fireplace could be used for heating food and water.

A stretcher table used for food-preparation chores in Daniel Boone's kitchen.

This gambrel-roofed Connecticut house was dismantled in 1953 and moved to Ohio, where it was reassembled. The building dates from 1778, but the kitchen section on the left had been a separate structure. It acquired a fireplace wall dating from 1754 during the rebuilding.

A sitting room in the gambrel-roofed house moved from Connecticut. A long-case clock from the 1770s is in the right corner.

Although it has been modernized considerably, the kitchen still retains the bare fireplace, which dates from 1754.

Eagle, Wisconsin, is the home of one of America's finest—and largest—outdoor living-history museums. Old World Wisconsin has a superb collection of rural buildings that mirror the life of Scandinavian, German, Polish, and African-American settlers as they built a life in the state.

Ninety miles away, a couple discovered an abandoned two-story settlers' cabin from 1846 that had spent most of the twentieth century covered with metal siding. The building was on the brink of demolition, and they acquired it, not knowing quite where it would end up, but sure that a place could be found. After numbering and tagging each of the 150-year-old logs, they stored it for two years until some woody acreage with abundant wildlife was found in Eagle. They rebuilt the house themselves.

The porch is large enough to be used for a number of activities.

A view of the kitchen dining area through to the porch.

In 1846 the metal bathtub would have been a relatively new and comfortable addition to a rustic cabin.

An upstairs bedroom is replete with vintage quilts and furniture.

Also in Eagle was a Greek revival farmhouse from 1841 that needed deconstruction. The history-loving new owners moved out of a recently built ranch-style house to work on their home, knowing that under the 1970s paneling and decor was the basic structure.

The original kitchen had been turned into a garage, so it had to be rebuilt. The evidence of life in the house 160 years ago is seen in a well-worn spot on the floor, where a rocking chair may have resided.

An old corner hutch fits neatly into a narrow hallway with period stencils on cream-colored walls.

Both the table and the hutch in the dining area date from the same mid-1800s period as the house. The yellowware in the hutch, although valuable, is sturdy enough to be used by the owners.

In the past, the area to one side of the kitchen doorway would have been called the buttery. The origin of this name derives not from any connection with dairy products but from from the French "botelerie," meaning a place for the storage of bottles, casks, and jars.

The cranberry-colored kitchen cupboards were made by the owner's brother.

Three views of the two-hundred-year-old split-log Virginia farmhouse seen on pages 45 and 87. The oak cupboard pictured above is from the same state and dates from the 1800s. The bold walls of the comfortable living room, shown on the right, easily absorb the varied shapes and colors of the sturdy furniture.

The lower of two porches that dominate one side of the house.

A cross-gabled, Cape-fronted Maine farmhouse was saved, made structurally sound, and enlarged with some innovative changes while retaining its original structural components. There were very few original internal details remaining, so it was decided to modernize the farmhouse rather than recreate its 1850s-era dark interiors. In place of the rickety old porch that covered half of one side of the building, a new one was built to go along most of the wall in front of the old kitchen windows. New openings were made in place of them, borrowing light that floods into the new white-painted and insulated porch. The sink and work surfaces are easily accessible from both porch and kitchen, creating a social and efficient section in that part of the farmhouse. The original unused and boarded-up front door became the restored back door and a new entryway was fashioned on the other side of the house between the kitchen block and a new gabled addition. After the restoration, the white Greek revival entablature and pilasters are emphasized by the color of the wall shingles.

The old boarded-up front entrance, and the new doorway.

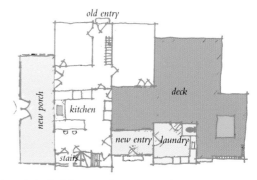

A rough sketch of the proposed renovations. The original portion of the house is unshaded.

The original porch was used as an entry to the house.

The side of the house before and after restoration.

The original narrow stairway was retained.

The original kitchen windows and the new openings.

A view of the porch through the opening of the kitchen wall in the 1850s Maine farmhouse.

A view of the white-painted porch.

The kitchen with its sink unit and opening to the porch. Exit to the porch is via the left of the counter in the foreground.

A side of the farmhouse with a deck on the same level as the original foundation.

The farmhouse at Kline Creek Farm at the Timber Ridge Forest Preserve in Winfield, Illinois, was the base of a working family farm in the 1960s, which was then purchased by the Forest Preserve District. Today it continues as the center of activity, but as a farmhouse operating in the manner of the period when it was built, in 1890. It is a living-history farm; throughout the farming year there are weekend programs that include everything from field to garden work—herding, planting, weeding, harvesting, canning, cooking, butter making, even doing laundry chores. There is great attention to detail and a fidelity to the proper use of all the tools and furnishings. There are many other activities including reenacted social occasions such as holidays, funerals, and weddings, as well as special events for Halloween and maple sugaring.

The attention to detail and the ambience of the 1890s is carefully maintained at the Kline Farmhouse. In the kitchen, the preserves are canned in jars of the period. At Christmas, the tree in the parlor has non-electric homemade decorations and the gifts have simple wrappings. The table is set with the best china and the napkins are folded in the form of Christmas crackers.

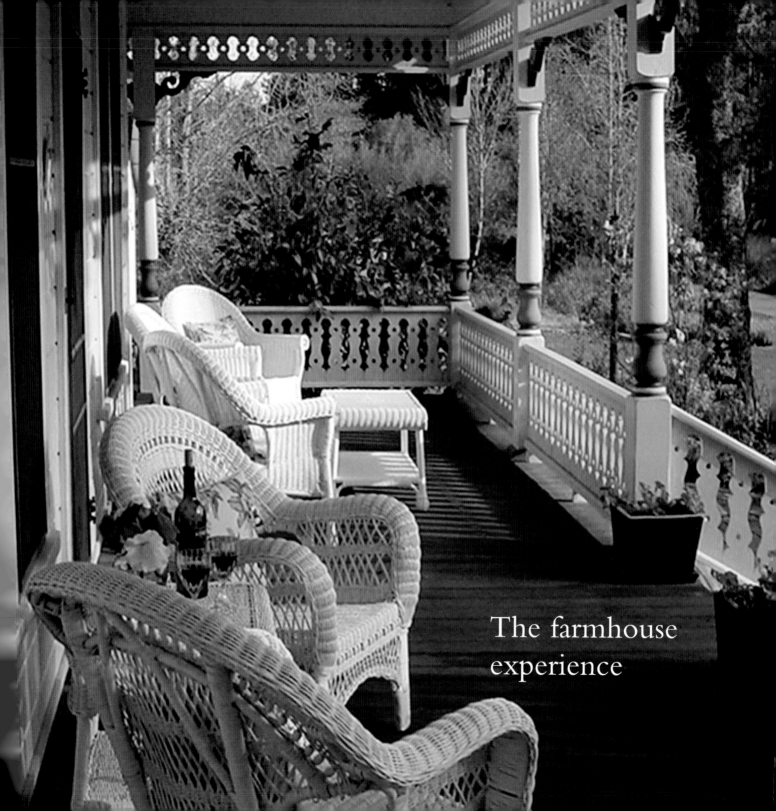

The farmhouse
experience

Above and left:
The Case Ranch.

Many of the farmhouses that appear in this book are faithfully preserved historic buildings or carefully restored homes. Some have been protected as a refuge from a city, and others to interpret history and to give people, especially nonfarmers, a sense of what they were like to live in. For people driving across rural North America, to stay in a farmhouse for a weekend as a paying guest is to experience something more than a diversion off an interstate route. There is a different pattern of living, and on a working farm, a simpler but active life. Here follows a small selection of welcoming places. Some are working farms that encourage participation in their activities, and some just evoke their past work and offer up the smells of hay and the earth. The emphasis here is on farmhouses that celebrate the original purposes of the buildings and in some cases are still in the hands of descendents of the families that originally built them. Some are prim and some are part of rambling compounds. There is not always a purity of style but they do tell of the characteristics of the region. They are not private like hotels, the doors may not always have locks, and the "hearty farmhouse breakfast" may be exaggerated or even absent, but now the long-abandoned farmhouse parlor will come into its own and be as important as the kitchen when hosts meet guests.

DeHaven

*DeHaven Valley Farm
39247 North
Highway 1,
Westport, California
95488*

*Telephone:
1 877 DEHAVEN
(334 2836)
or 707 961 1660*

*E-mail:
info@dehavenvalleyfarm.
com*

*Website:
www.dehaven-valley-
farm.com*

DeHaven was built in 1875 by the members of the Gordon family, who moved to California from Canada. It was the manor house for a one-thousand-acre sheep and cattle ranch. To the east was the town of DeHaven, population three hundred, built and owned by the Pollard Lumber Company. The town was originally named by settlers from Holland; DeHaven is Dutch for "harbor." To the immediate south was the town of Westport, population three thousand, the largest coastal town north of San Francisco and an important shipping port with its two logging chutes (they were the longest in California).

But life proved too difficult on this part of the coast. The owner of the ranch and manor house moved his cattle farther south. Shortly after, the lumber company shut down; the town was ultimately destroyed by a fire in 1920. The coastline rocks were too treacherous for ships despite the length of the chutes, and the train bypassed Westport for the (then) small army outpost, Fort Bragg. Westport's church twice slid off the cliff into the ocean and most people moved away to find work.

In the early 1930s, the farmhouse's owners began serving dinners and allowed guests to stay the night (for an additional fee of three dollars). The concept quickly took hold as guests began coming from as far away as San Francisco to experience the splendor of the "Lost Coast," a sixty-mile-long wilderness. Today Westport is a quiet village, population 238, and the original DeHaven manor house still stands next to the Pacific Ocean, surrounded by twenty acres of meadows, rolling hills, trees, and pastures. People from all over the world come to stay. The owners are committed to preparing exceptional cuisine and supporting sustainable agriculture and organic farming, and the chef uses the farmhouse garden and local ingredients to plan her menu.

Howard Creek Ranch

Snuggled in a valley along California's scenic Mendocino Coast, this New England–style farmhouse, dating from 1871, may seem like it's on the wrong side of the country. The antique-strewn inn still has its original parlor fireplace

Howard Creek before restoration; opposite, the ranch today.

and even the home's original bathtub. One, Lucy's Room, features a century-old window-pane with "Lucy Howard" etched in the glass.

Howard Creek Ranch is alive with the rural splendor of sweeping ocean and mountain views, forty acres of peace and beauty on the beach near the "Lost Coast." The ranch was settled in 1867 as a land grant of thousands of acres and included a sheep and cattle ranch. Today, horses, cows, sheep, and llamas graze the pastures. The buildings are constructed from virgin redwood from the nearby forest.

Breakfast is cooked on the old wood stoves. A seventy-five-foot swinging bridge takes guests across Howard Creek to the carriage house; the creek flows past barns and cabins to the beach two hundred yards away. Rooms have large, comfortable beds, handmade quilts, private decks, balconies, fireplaces or wood-stoves, musical instruments, books, and ocean, mountain, or creek views, with direct beach access. There are prize-winning flower gardens and the amenities include those that are unmis-takably "California," including a sauna, swim-ming pool, wood-heated hot tub, and a massage service.

The accommodations here also include sepa-rate redwood cabins, the most unusual being the Boat House, built around the hull and gal-ley of a boat. This cabin is also located beside a creek that is lit at night.

There are wild deer, a bobcat, a fox family, raccoons, and occasionally a porcupine, elk, mountain lion, and bear. The owners have cleared Howard Creek of logjams and the Department of Fish and Game has restocked the creek with salmon.

*Howard Creek Ranch
40501 North
Highway 1,
(PO Box 121)
Westport, California
95488
Telephone:
707 964 6725
Website:
www.howardcreekranch.com*

Case Ranch

*Case Ranch Inn
Bed and Breakfast
7446 Poplar Drive,
Forestville, California
95436
Telephone:
707 887 8711
Fax: 707 887 8607
Toll free:
1 877 887 8711
E-mail:
diana@caseranchinn.com
Website:
www.caseranchinn.com*

Built circa 1894 by Joseph Walker, the Case Ranch was purchased by James L. Case in 1910. At that time, it consisted of a Victorian farmhouse on fifty acres in the rolling hills of the Russian River Valley, in Sonoma County, California; apples were the reigning crop. Mr. Case, a Methodist minister, was an active voice in the farm labor movement, and the Case Ranch was the center of much protest activity during the Great Depression.

A century later, the Russian River Valley now produces high-quality wine rather than apples, and the Case Ranch sits on two acres on a quiet country road surrounded by original fruit trees. The farmhouse has a particularly fine wraparound porch, an authentically restored parlor, and very comfortable bedroom suites. It is a registered Sonoma County Historical Landmark.

*Palo Alto Creek Farm
Bed and Breakfast
231 West Main,
Fredericksburg, Texas
78624
Telephone:
800 997 0089
Fax: 830 997 8282
E-mail:
gasthaus@ktc.com
Website:
www.paloaltocreekfarm.com*

The turn-of-the-twentieth-century dining room at the Case Ranch.

Palo Alto Creek Farm

The Fredericksburg roads in the Texas hill country are almost entirely traffic-free and are ideal for walking, jogging, or biking. The Palo Alto Creek Farm has two historic buildings with accommodations, both with their own spa facilities.

The Barn is an 1880s limestone structure that originally housed livestock. It has been meticulously renovated to provide guests with self-contained country comfort. Large glass windows, formerly the doors through which animals entered and exited the building, provide a panoramic view of the ancient live oak trees and lawns that slope down to the creek. A private, vine-covered lattice porch beckons you to enter.

Inside there are rustic pine floors of old wood that have absorbed the strength of the work of many generations, as well as ancient rock walls that are sixteen inches thick. There are antiques and folk art, including an original lightning rod from the Karl Itz farmhouse.

The restored log-cabin farmhouse on the property was built shortly after Karl ltz and his bride, Henrietta Evers, settled here in the early

1850s. The first ltz family raised eight children in the building. There is a front porch with rocking chairs, and inside the original field-stone is still in use. It has a particularly interesting bathroom with a kiva fireplace.

Sakura Ridge

Sakura Ridge is a working organic orchard with bed-and-breakfast accommodation located on a south slope in the foothills of Mount Hood, Oregon. The farm grows Oregon's organic dark sweet cherries and delicate pears. Active guests who want to experience the work and harvest are invited to participate—they are supplied with gardening tools or picking buckets. Others may prefer to relax in rockers and enjoy the outstanding panoramic views.

Sakura Ridge
The Farm and Lodge
5601 York Hill Drive,
Hood River, Oregon
97031
Telephone:
1 877 4 SAKURA
Website:
www.sakuraridge.com

The guest house at the Sakura Ridge working farm.

One of the bedrooms at Sakura Ridge.

A recent news release reported:

Spring brings 6,000 trees in bloom as well as all the asparagus you can pick and eat. Now is the time of year for 30 tons of organic composted chicken fertilizer. This is a volunteers-only job. We'll give you the gloves. Join us in the summer for our 80-ton cherry harvest destined for the Sakura Ridge breakfast table, as well as markets all around the world. We have a picking bucket just for you. From labor day through october, garden harvests of heirloom tomatoes, squash, pumpkins and more await you. Don't forget, we still have to pick 3,000 pear trees.

*Bluff Creek Inn
Bed and Breakfast
1161 Bluff Creek
Drive, Chaska,
Minnesota
55318*

*Telephone:
800 445 6958 or
952 445 2735*

*Website:
bluffcreekbb.com*

Bluff Creek Inn

The property deed for this Minnesota farm-house was signed by President Abraham Lincoln, and is on display in its parlor. The home was built in 1860 with local yellow Chaska bricks. Four years earlier, a settler from Vermont named Lucian Howe arrived in the area. He knew how to convert to brick the multiple natural deposits of quality clay within the bounds of Chaska. He established a brick-yard and by 1857 produced the bricks for the first such house built in Carver County. Today the farmhouse has five guest rooms, and the long front porch is an especially charming loca-tion for wedding ceremonies.

Turtleback Farm Inn

Turtleback Farm Inn
1981 Crow Valley
Road, Eastsound
Orcas Island,
Washington 98245

Telephone:
800 376 4914 or
360 376 4914
Fax:
360 376 5329
E-mail:
info@turtlebackinn.com

Turtleback Farm Inn is a country farmhouse located on Orcas Island, one the loveliest of the San Juan Islands that dot Puget Sound. The house was built in the late 1800s and expanded in 1985. The parlor has a Rumford fireplace. This graceful and comfortable inn has seven bedrooms, each with a private bathroom and decorated with a blend of fine antiques and contemporary pieces. The addition of the very private Orchard House, with four large bedrooms that each have full bathrooms and private decks, adds another dimension to the complex. This architecturally interesting farmhouse with fine accommodations is worth a special trip to the island.

The Inn at Locke House

There is a well documented history of the Locke farmhouse. In 1855 Dr. Dean Jewett Locke of New Hampshire brought his bride, Delia Hammond of Massachusetts, to his homestead in the San Joaquin Valley of California. They built a small frame house which was replaced by a three-story brick structure in 1865. A water tower was constructed in 1881, and a two-story addition built in 1882. Soon the house accommodated the Lockes' thirteen children, relatives, visitors, and sometimes patients. Here Dr. Locke conducted his medical practice as well as other businesses. Both the house and barn were centers for the pioneer community of Lockeford, which he generously supported until his death. Today, the complex is on the National Register of Historic Places and shows many examples of its New England neo-Georgian roots in its vernacular makeup combining the history of the local community with its founder Dr. Locke. Inside the farmhouse that now functions as a relaxing and comfortable inn, one catches an evocation of the home in the last quarter of the nineteenth century—particularly in its restored, memento-filled parlor that must have been the site of many special occasions when small feet kept the pump organ going.

The inn's gardens supply a bounty of ingredients for the ever-changing menu. The brick barn is worth visiting on a walk around the fruit-tree-filled grounds. There are four guest rooms and a suite in the water tower. All have full bathrooms and fireplaces.

Two views of the parlor at Locke House.

The Inn at Locke House
19960 North Elliot
Road, PO Box 1510
Lockeford, California
95237

Telephone:
209 727 5715
E-mail:
lockehouse@jps.net
Website:
theinnatlockehouse.com

Eastfield

Historic Eastfield in Rennselaer County, New York, is the unique creation and life work of Don Carpentier. Since 1958 he has been collecting and reconstructing the stuff of everyday life between the years 1787 and 1840. The village is called Eastfield because Carpentier's father gave him eight acres of woodlot near the east field of the family farm in 1971 for the first of his reconstructions: a blacksmith's shop (somebody's pigpen before Don dismantled and hauled it there). Eastfield now has more than twenty rural buildings, including a large tavern. The point of Eastfield is participation and education. Although its programs cover much more than farmhouse history, anyone seriously interested in rural skills and life would find a stay rewarding. Recently there were workshops for domestic skills and trades that covered early American lighting, ceramics restoration, everyday textiles, fireplace and oven building, tinsmithing, and more. According to the Historic Eastfield brochure:

Students are involved in actual preservation work and have the experience of working first-hand with the tools and materials of the trades taught. The depth and detail of the courses are unique to Eastfield, as many of the courses are five-days long. The emphasis is not on lectures, and the working craftsmen who teach the courses are available to answer specific questions and problems at every level.

The lure of Eastfield is more than its curriculum. Students that are taking the classes at the Village are encouraged to live there during their courses. This offers a special opportunity to understand the daily lives, as well as the work, of the tradesmen of the pre-industrial age. Meals may be cooked in the late-eighteenth-century kitchen. Accommodations are rope beds with straw and feather ticks. Eastfield offers an opportunity to be with others—students and teachers—of similar interests.

One of the most intriguing facets of Eastfield's workshops is the experience of living in the Village during the class. Lodging in Eastfield's taverns is available free of charge for those wishing to stay in early-nineteenth-century accommodations. The only requirement is that each person supply ten 10-inch white candles.

Food is the individual's responsibility. For those wishing to prepare their own meals, cooking can be done in the tavern's fireplace and brick oven. Those who prefer can purchase their meals locally.

Since there is no charge for staying in the Village after daily sessions, you are our guests and are therefore expected to pitch in with chores and cleanup. This may include carrying firewood and water, washing dishes, sweeping floors, etc. Bedding is the responsibility of each guest. There is a large pond for washing and swimming.

Eastfield Village: Box 465, Nassau, New York 12123

Telephone: 518 766 2422

E-mail: dcsapottery1@taconic.net

A small historic farmhouse at Eastfield.

Washburn-Norlands

In the same participatory mode but with less stress on crafts skills and more of an emphasis on the involvement of children, there is the hands-on experience of nineteenth-century rural Maine farm life that is offered at the Washburn-Norlands Living History Center. For two days and nights, visitors experience the ebb and flow of daily life as they role-play members of a nineteenth-century farm family in the beautiful setting of the Washburn family home. As members of the family, they help with farm chores, cooking, and cleaning, and the children play games of the period and attend school. There is also the opportunity to delve more deeply into the background of the assumed characters, and explore the historic buildings.

This is a structured program under the full-time supervision of the center's staff. It is expected that minors will be accompanied by an adult. Live-in participants should be open to trying all the new experiences. Here, the visitor is an active participant in daily and seasonal farming and housework, and he or she becomes involved in the social, political, and educational activities of the times.

The emphasis is on the frugal lifestyle of the northern New England farm family, as expressed in a "use it up, wear it out, make it do, or do without" philosophy. While there was little leisure for a farm family, some free time is scheduled. This is living history, so sleeping accommodations are old-fashioned bunk-house style and bathroom facilities are chamber pots and privies.

Washburn-Norlands encompasses 445 acres of land and six nineteenth-century buildings on their original sites. Among these are the Victorian mansion of the Washburn family, with the attached farmer's cottage and large barn that houses farm animals—draft horses, oxen, milk cows, sheep, pigs, and chickens— typical of the livestock owned by an 1870s farming family. The barn also contains many examples of nineteenth- and early-twentieth-century farm tools. These are used in the daily operation of the farm and to teach agricultural history in the hands-on educational programs. The land, buildings, and contents present an outstanding microcosm of nineteenth-century rural New England life and provide invaluable tools for understanding and appreciating the past and its relationship to the present.

Washburn-Norlands Living History Center 290 Norlands Road, Livermore, Maine 04253 Telephone: 207 897 4366 Fax: 207 897 4963 E-mail: norlands@norlands.org

Part of the farmhouse and connected barn at Washburn-Norlands.

Farmhouse preservation

New owners of farmhouses who are interested in history are likely to be concerned about the future of their homes. What can be done to retain a farmhouse's integrity as people's lifestyles change? Decisions will have to be made—sometimes they will be controversial. Until the twentieth century the North American farmhouse gradually evolved, grew in size, was rebuilt on the same site, or sometimes moved down the road to suit the changing needs of farming families. And as the working rural population shrank, the age of restoration arrived. I have noticed that what often kept the feeling of an old building alive was the thrift of the succeeding generations of the families who lived there. They repaired and patched the home, gradually adding to its history. But many of the succeeding owners had more money than intelligent ways of preservation, and many authentic details were destroyed or removed, with unfortunate results—from guesswork when a later set of residents attempted to "bring it back." Bring it back to when? What interpretation of its past would be right? Early farmhouses had smaller window panes, and by the middle of the nineteenth century farmwives were grateful when the same frame was filled with a single sheet of glass; porches were added and chimneys were rebuilt for new efficient stoves, and so on. They were all changed in some way. It's best to pick a date that typifies the farmhouse. Outdoor living-history museums often stop their interpretive clocks at a time when the buildings were in their most active periods. Plimoth Plantation depicts the houses as they were seven years after the landing. Shaker village life is shown when the Shakers were in their heyday in 1840; Old Sturbridge Village depicts life about eight or so years earlier; and Colonial Williamsburg revisits 1774. In larger, more expansive rural-life museums like Living History Farms in Iowa and Old World Wisconsin, farmhouses are shown in the years when immigrants arrived and built the farms. A farm museum interpreting its period rooms would choose an as-accurate-as-possible date.

The future of rural homes

The most valuable thing on a farm has always been the land, and the future of many older farmhouses has become secondary to the acreage that is sold off as the family farm continues to disappear. The Industrial Revolution pulled people away from the farm, as the amount of labor necessary to work the land was reduced and there was more work to be found in the cities. Now, the age of mass communications and computers is providing an opportunity to return to rural living. With a well-equipped home office, work can take place virtually anywhere in an existing farmstead that has been cared for. And while an occasional trip into the city may be necessary, it also may not. The benefits of such an arrangement are not measured simply in time and money. People with an appreciation for history who live in reused farmhouses in rural areas find them good places to raise children, with relatively uncrowded schools and a healthy environment.

But unless something more is done to protect these historic structures, somebody, somewhere will find a reason to demolish them.

In the United States, the American Farmland Trust and similar state trusts struggle to keep farmland in the domain of agriculture, not development, but it's uphill work. Today less than 3 percent of all Americans live on farms; much of the rural landscape in America is one of abandonment and desolation. For the past fifteen years in upstate New York, one thousand farms per year have gone out of business. James Howard Kunstler, describing the scourge of rampant development, writes in *Home from Nowhere*, " . . . these days, farmers consider the land to be their retirement fund. They hope to attract buyers who will pay a price commensurate with its presumed 'development value' that is, as a cul-de-sac housing subdivision or worse. Most farmers don't hit the jackpot, of course, and so many corners of New York State that used to be primarily agricultural are returning to forest. This is not the worst thing that could happen to farmland, but in terms of history and culture it represents a tragic waste of investment, since most of this land was originally cleared with great effort." He believes we are going to need the remaining farmland around our towns and cities. Right now, much of New York farmland that is not close to a major highway or a tourist town is undervalued.

Within commutable distances of the prosperous cities most of the charming farmhouses have been snapped up; for those still looking, it's a race between them and developers to secure a place on at least some of a farm's original acreage. But what has happened to the descendants of the original farming families? Where are they going to live? They certainly can't afford anything that looks like the old family home. Events like this have helped to develop the New American Vernacular—a sad sight on the rural landscape. It comes down the road preceded by a pickup with blinking amber lights and an *Oversize Load* banner across its hood. The prefabricated building, or one long half of it, rests on the trailing portion of an eighteen-wheeler. The white- or pastel-tinted exposed side is completely vinyl, its molding faked to look like clapboarding, and the windows are flanked by glued-on imitation shutters that attempt to break up the monotony of its flat, single-storied length. It will come to rest on a concrete foundation, often on a portion of the land that a farming family has not yet sold off—the original farmhouse gone or now occupied by weekenders. It is said that just under 40 percent of the rural population in the southern states live in mobile homes—mobile in the act of delivery only.

And on farmland that has been sold off for development there are the fake "architect designed" farmhouses that come "ready to use," influenced by many of the styles illustrated in this book—except that at first glance one sees them as double garages. The gaping mouth of the garage cannot quite hide the Cape, the Dutch, the saltbox, and the French colonial influences that appear on groomed sites, where few people

walk between them. There are no sidewalks.

Symbols are important in these new rural "communities" that are quickly being built

everywhere. The old pineapple motifs are replaced by the plastic eagle over the garage doors. For many years, Americans have had a deeply held belief that Greek- and Roman-looking classical columns and pediments lend dignity and a sense of success and power to the front of a farmhouse. At first this was done with wood imitating stone, and now the builders imitate wood with vinyl, literally tacked on (often with a brad nailer, which is fired with a burst of pressurized air). These houses are built without affection because they are no longer lived in by those who built them.

According to Kunstler: "The tragic thing is that there existed in America a fine heritage of regional home-building traditions, rich with values and meanings, and we threw it all away. Vestigial symbols of that tradition remain—the screw-on plastic shutters, fanlights with pop-in mullions, vinyl clapboards, the fakey front portico too narrow to put a chair on—but the building culture from which these details derive is as lost as the music of the Aztecs."

Lastly Kunstler presents a fascinating paradox of culture: "The better our power tools get, and the more clever our systemization of assembly becomes, the worse our houses look." I'm with him.

In earlier times, such as the 1930s, more attention was paid to a region's architectural heritage. Up and down the Taconic Parkway on the east side of the Hudson Valley in New York, the Works Progress Administration (WPA) with the Civilian Conservation Corps (CCC) built filling stations in a variety of Dutch farmhouse styles with fine details. In Dutchess County one sits on an island, unused but preserved, between opposing traffic lanes.

What can be done to preserve the values represented by the farmhouse? Architect Frank Lloyd Wright, a second-generation descendant of an immigrant Welsh farming family, installed a working hearth in every one of his radical house designs as the focus of any living area. For an educational project city children living in apartments were asked to draw a house. Without exception they each drew an isolated cottage with two windows, a center door, and smoke curling up from a chimney on the roof. It seems that the hearth and home have not been abandoned completely, even with modern houses with traditional exterior elements but with contemporary accoutrements such as Jacuzzis, sunrooms, game rooms, television dens, exercise rooms, and dining room/ kitchens. Though these modern interior spaces are relatively doorless, harkening back to the original farmhouse layout, they have fake fireplaces.

Wright gave us the open plan, but was not much interested in kitchens except that they be efficient, and his galleylike designs follow from when women began to lay out plans for progressive farmhouses. Wright's kitchens were small with some storage compartments, and were not welcoming. Food preparation was seen to be a separate chore and not a family activity. Thankfully things have changed, with a gesture back to earlier times with the combined large kitchen and eating areas, and now with clever wall partitions between the two zones. They almost go far enough to conceal the notion that eating is a pleasure and cooking is work. What could recreate the farmhouse feeling in a modern house in the country is when all the family activities—talking, working, baking, celebrating—take place in one big room with a big table and comfortable chairs scattered around. It would be good to have a door that leads out directly to the kitchen garden and large enough windows through which to check on the produce being grown.

Better a home like this than an old farmhouse in which the decor has been faked by a decorator (now called interior designer) and houses the collections of "stuff" gathered on weekends—a private museum of ordinary rural artifacts that are now too valuable to actually use—like a collection of copper jelly molds tacked to the wall, bird decoys arranged on an early-nineteenth-century dresser with newly distressed paintwork, or a forest of artisans' baskets hanging from iron butchers' hooks. These tableaux, described by the antique-dealing Keno brothers as "decorative ensembles," are the props that sell the shelter magazines and raise the price of property.

Large cities are now beginning to come to grips with their original purpose: offering a choice of housing to those whose incomes, lifestyles, ages, and cultures vary widely. There seems to be no similar strategy for rural towns and the surrounding farmland; the people who buy country homes are becoming suburbanized by our car culture, and zoning laws are all over the place if they exist at all. If farmhouses are saved, they can continue to represent the history of their original builders and owners, and also the occupants who followed them over the years. If the land they sit on can be made agriculturally or ecologically sound, so much the better.

Glossary

abacus: In classical architecture, the flat slab topping a capital.

Adam: The style period from 1765–1790. The Adam brothers introduced the neoclassical style in furniture and architecture to England.

adobe: Unbaked clay brick, dried by the sun, introduced by the Spanish settlers for house-building in the southwestern United States.

applique ornament: Usually carved wood, fastened to a surface of a building.

apron: A horizontal cross member or framing element used below a chair seat, tabletop, or the under-structure of a case piece; it is often shaped along the lower edge for decorative effect. It is also known as a skirt.

arcade: A line of arches supported by columns forming a roofed passageway.

arch: A curved structure made of wedge-shaped stones or bricks, spanning an opening and capable of bearing the weight of the material above it.

architrave: The shaped frame around a door or window opening; in classical architecture, the lowest member of an entablature.

armchair: A dining chair with arms (properly called an open armchair). Also, loosely, any chair with arms.

ashlar: Square-edged blocks of stone, laid horizontally and joined vertically to form walls.

atrium: A light-filled hall or court located in the center of a building.

ax helve: The wooden handle of an ax.

back splat: The central support of a chair back.

back stool: Literally, a joint stool with a back; the earliest form of a side chair.

bake-kettle: A cast iron kettle with a tight-fitting, flat lid used for baking small amounts of food. The bake-kettle is set over a bed of coals and another bed of coals is laid on top of the lid, producing heat from both top and bottom for even baking.

balloon frame: A simplified method of timberframe construction, avoiding interior supports, that became popular in the United States during the late nineteenth and early twentieth centuries.

baluster: An upright, usually turned, vertical support of a stair rail, table, or chair; often with a vase-shaped outline.

balustrade: A handrail supported by a series of balusters or pillars.

banking: Pushing raked-up leaves against the foundation of the house to keep out cold and drafts.

bargeboard: A wide, flat board that seals the space below the roof, between the tiles and the wall, on a gable end. Bargeboards often have decorative carving or pierced decoration. It is also called a vergeboard.

baroque: The bold architectural style of the late Renaissance that followed the unrestrained mannerist style and is characterized by exuberant but organized decoration and composition.

barrel vault: A straight, continuous arched vault or ceiling in tunnel form, either semicircular or semi-elliptical in profile.

battlement: A notched wall at the top of a medieval-style building, originally for the purpose of fortification.

bay window: A projection with a window on a house facade. It may be curved (bow window) or angular in plan.

bed: A sack filled with feathers or straw.

bed bench (or bed settle): A wooden bench or settle whose box-like seat opened out to form a bed.

bed hangings: Curtains surrounding a four-poster bed that not only ensured warmth and privacy but also displayed the family's wealth and good taste. Bed hangings were among the most expensive linens in a colonial household.

bed pole: Either the poles running between the tops of the bed posts to support the hangings, or a long-handled paddle used for smoothing the sheets when making a bed, kept in the corner of a room.

bed steps: A set of two or three steps, sometimes with a compartment for a chamber pot, to help people who were old, infirm, or short get in and out of high beds.

bed warmer: A long-handled brass or copper pan that held hot coals for warming the bed; called a warming pan in England (*see also* warming pan).

bedding-down candle: A short candle that burned for only fifteen or twenty minutes and extinguished itself after one had gone to bed. The stub ends of regular candles were often used in this way.

bedmoss: A fibrous growth on trees, sometimes called Spanish moss, used for bed stuffing.

bedstead: The frame of the bed.

bedstead-washstand: A piece of furniture resembling a secretary, in which the "desk" opened to a washstand, and the "bookcase" to a bed. An extreme example of Victorian ingenuity, but there were many like it, showing that even by the end of the nineteenth century, living rooms were still slept in.

beetle: Heavy wooden hammer.

bellows: A tool for producing a strong current of air, used for blowing fires or sounding a pipe organ.

berm: An artificially created mound of soil or earth.

berry spoon: A dessert-size spoon with fruit embossed on the bowl (many Georgian spoons have Victorian embossing). Used for eating fruit.

blanket chest: An American term for a lift-top chest with drawers underneath.

bonnet top: A broken-arch pediment backed by boards.

borning room: A room off the kitchen or keeping room used for the birth of babies and care of the sick.

boulter: A sifter.

bracket foot: A support formed by two pieces of wood that join at the corner.

breakfast table: A small movable table with drop leaves or a rectangular tilting top on a tripod base.

breakfront: A protruding central section.

breezeway: A roofed passage open at the sides between separate buildings.

bressumer: A large horizontal beam that spans a fireplace or other opening.

broach: To put on the spit for cooking purposes.

broken-arch pediment: A roughly triangular-shaped top patterned by opposing S-shaped arches that remain open at the apex; found on American tall-case furniture of the mid-eighteenth century.

broken pediment: A pediment in which one or both cornices are not continuous; a gap in the crown, sometimes filled with an urn or another motif.

bureau: A low desk or writing table with drawers.

buttery: A small room for storing bottles and food containers; from the French word *botelerie*.

cabriole leg: An S-shaped furniture leg on which the knee curves out and the ankle curves in, ending in an ornamental foot.

candlestand: A small stand, usually on a tripod base and easily movable, to hold a candlestick.

cantilever: A projecting beam that is supported at one end only. It usually supports a structure, like a balcony, where supports cannot be placed or are not desired.

capital: The top part of a column, usually decorated, and larger than the shaft of the column.

card or game table: A small folding table at which four people could sit. Used for playing cards or other games. Often with a fold-over top. A very common form of table in the eighteenth and nineteenth centuries.

carding: The process of brushing the wool fibers to untangle and align them in the same direction prior to spinning.

cartouche: A decorative scroll or shield-shaped ornamental panel.

chamber pot: A bedroom vessel for urination and defecation, used to avoid trips outside during the night.

Charles II or Restoration: The style period after the Cromwellian Protectorate (1660–1680). King Charles II brought French taste back to England following his exile from England to the French court. Characterized by the use of walnut, although oak is still prominent.

chest: A large storage box with lid, designed to stand on the floor. The earliest form of storage, common from the seventeenth century onward.

chest on chest: A two-part case piece with both parts containing three or four layers of drawers and standing on low feet or a base.

chest of drawers (commonly referred to, incorrectly, as a dresser): A chest fitted with drawers.

chest on stand (*see also* highboy): A two-part case piece consisting of a chest of drawers on a separate stand that may have one drawer in it or be raised on short legs.

cheval glass: A full-length mirror fitted on a four-legged frame with crossbars and flanking uprights, which allows it to tilt.

Chippendale: English furniture style named after Thomas Chippendale, designer and cabinetmaker whose book *The Director*, published in 1754, influenced the direction of English (and American) taste.

clapboard (pronounced *kla'berd*): A thin board that, when laid horizontally and overlapped, creates a weather-tight outer wall surface on a timberframed building.

classical: Having to do with the style of the ancient Greek or Roman periods.

claw-and-ball foot: A foot carved in the form of an animal or bird claw grasping a ball.

colonnade: A series of columns supporting arches.

column: A vertical member consisting of a nearly cylindrical shaft, with a base and capital used as a support or building ornament.

Composite: A classical order in architecture where columns combine Corinthian acanthus leaves with Ionic scrolls.

corbel: A projecting stone or timber block supporting a horizontal member such as a beam.

Corinthian: The latest and most ornate of the classical orders of architecture. The column is slender and usually fluted, the capital elaborately carved with acanthus leaves.

corner chair: A chair with a semicircular back around two sides. In the period, often called desk chair or smoking chair, and rarely set in a corner. An eighteenth-century form.

corner washstand (*see also* washstand): A triangular washstand designed to stand in the corner of a bedroom.

cornice: An ornamental crowning, typically molded; similar to the top of an entablature in architecture that projects along the top of a wall, pillar, side of a building, or a piece of case furniture.

court cupboard: A sixteenth- and seventeenth-century storage and display piece that may be open or enclosed, usually heavily carved.

coverlid: Coverlet; cloth that is spread over all the other coverings of a bed.

crane: A horizontal iron arm in a fireplace for supporting kettles, usually hinged to swing away from the fire in order to adjust temperature or provide access to kettles.

credence table: A seventeenth-century side table with folding top, often semicircular or hexagonal in form.

crenellation: A pattern of square indentations that are often called battlements.

cresting: An ornamental finish, usually made of wood or metal, at the top of a building, such as the ridge of a roof.

crest rail: The top horizontal rail of a chair, settee, or sofa.

cricket: A small, low stool.

Cromwellian: The style period of Puritan rule from 1640–1660. Characterized by a severity and absence of unnecessary decoration.

cruse: A small cup. In New England, the term was used for a small bottle to hold vinegar.

cupola: A dome, usually small, topping a roof or turret, that lets light or air into a building.

curd: The thickened part of milk, which is formed into cheese.

cutter: A light sleigh.

cyma curve: An S-shaped or double-curved line, one half of which is concave, the other half of which is convex.

dado: The lower wall surface, from the chair rail down to the skirting board.

demilune: Semicircular, or half-moon, shape.

desk and bookcase: A tall case piece that includes an upper section fitted with shelves and partitions for books and papers, and a lower section that includes a writing surface, often with drawers or cabinet doors below. It is also known as a secretary-bookcase.

dished top: A tabletop, often hewn from a single board, that features a shallow raised run.

dog-leg stair: Two flights of stairs parallel to each other with a half landing in between.

Doric: The earliest and plainest of the classical orders. Doric columns usually have no base; the shaft is thick and broadly fluted, the capital spare and unornamented.

dormer: An upright window that projects from a sloping roof.

dresser (often Welsh dresser; *see also* low dresser): A two-part country piece. The top consists of shelves for storage and display of plates and other dishes; the lower part has drawers and sometimes doors. Besides being used for storage, it was used to "dress" food just before it was served.

drop leaf: A hinged extension that is attached to the stationary top of a table so that it can be folded down when not in use.

Early Georgian (George I and II): The style period from 1715–1760. Characterized by the increasing use of mahogany and the introduction of Chippendale style.

earthen: clay; in New England this was a gray clay that fired to a red color; sometimes referred to as redware.

easy chair: An upholstered armchair with a winged high back and enclosed padded arms. It is also known as a wing chair.

eaves: The lower edge of a roof that projects beyond the wall underneath.

eel grass: A submerged, long-leaved marine plant that grows abundantly along the Atlantic coast. The stems are used for woven products, such as mats or hats.

elevation: The external face of a building.

entablature: The part of a classical building resting on the top of columns, made up of an architrave, frieze, and cornice.

escutcheon: The plate around a keyhole.

fall front: The hinged cover of a desk or secretary that folds out to form a writing surface.

fanlight: A semicircular window above a door, with glazing radiating out like a fan or sunburst. It is sometimes called a transom window.

farm table: A country table with a solid top and no drop leaves, usually rectangular in shape.

federal: The style period from 1790–1830; specific to American furniture and architecture. Derived from Hepplewhite and Sheraton and, toward the end of the period, from French empire.

fenestration: The arrangement of windows in a building.

figure: The grain pattern displayed on a cut piece of wood.

finial: An ornament on top of a spire, roof, post, or canopy.

fireback: A decorated iron plate at the back of a fireplace that protects the wall and reflects heat.

Flemish bond: A form of brickwork in which, on each course, headers and stretchers alternate.

flummery: Fruit pudding; some were thin like soup while others were thick. Some were simply cooked fruit thickened with cornstarch, while others included ingredients such as lemons, sugar, milk, eggs, and isinglass.

fluting: Decorative carving in the form of grooves derived from Classical columns.

four-poster: A bed with four tall corner posts that may or may not support a tester.

fretwork: A form of openwork or low-relief carving that resembles a geometric grid pattern or latticework.

frieze: A flat or sculpted ornamental band on furniture; it runs horizontally, such as on the apron of a table or on the area that is beneath a pediment molding.

gable: That part of the wall immediately under the end of a pitched roof, cut into a triangular shape by the sloping sides of the roof.

gambrel roof: A roof with a double pitch, resembling a mansard roof.

gateleg table: A table with two drop leaves that are supported on swinging "gates," which pivot from the frame and stretchers (top and bottom) of the table.

George III: The style period from 1760–1820. The rise of the wealthy middle class resulted in a huge growth in the furniture industry; thus, more examples of late Georgian furniture survive than from any prior period. Styles from this period include Sheraton, Hepplewhite, Regency, and Adam (see individual definitions).

gesso: Plaster mixed with a binding material; it is used for relief work or as a ground for painting or gilding.

gilding: To coat with a thin layer of gold or a gold-colored paint.

gingerbread: Ornate wood decoration used in Victorian-style buildings.

girandole: A branched candleholder with a backplate fixed to a wall or overmantel.

girt: A horizontal supporting beam.

gridiron: A grate for broiling food over coals.

grist: Grain that has been ground into flour.

half-landing: A landing halfway up a flight of stairs.

half-timber: A type of construction in which spaces formed by a timber frame are filled in with stone, bricks, or wattle and daub, the frame left exposed.

handkerchief table: A triangular table with a triangular drop leaf that becomes square when the leaf is raised.

harvest table: A long narrow table with two narrow drop leaves supported on pull-out lopers.

header: A brick laid so that only its short face is visible.

Hepplewhite: The style period from 1780–1795, named after the author of the widely influential *Cabinetmaker and Upholsterer's Guide*, published in 1788.

highboy: A two-part case piece, the upper consisting of three or four layers of drawers, the lower of one or two layers of drawers raised on legs.

high chest: A tall, two-part case piece consisting of an upper case with drawers that rest on top of a lower section, also with drawers, that is raised on legs.

high pan: A cooking pot raised up on three built-in legs so that a fire could be built under it.

hired-man's bed: A narrow, slatted bed, often spool-turned, produced in quantity by factories in the Midwest and New England between about 1840 and 1890. Despite its name, it was designed as cottage furniture, not for servants.

incising: A carving technique in which a fine, sharp instrument is used to produce a lined pattern.

inglenook: A recessed space beside a fireplace, usually housing a bench.

inlay: Ornamentation of Flemish origin that involves the skillful insertion of patterned material (such as wood veneers) into the surface.

intaglio: Low-relief decorative carving.

Ionic: One of the classical orders of architecture, characterized by fluted columns and prominent volutes on the capitals.

iron furnace: A cast iron brazier; a cast iron pot that holds hot coals and in which food is exposed to the heat over a grill; used to create a fire away from the fireplace or hearth.

isinglass: Gelatin for thickening.

Jacobean: Loosely used to refer to the style period from the seventeenth century.

joint stool: A stool made with mortise-and-tenon joints (as opposed to a boarded-and-nailed stool). The most common piece of furniture in sixteenth- and seventeenth-century houses.

joist: Intermediate parallel beams that support a floor or ceiling.

keeler: A broad, shallow tub.

keeping room: A room used for all family activities, and as a bedchamber for parents and very young children.

keystone: The central stone in the curve of an arch or vault.

leaded lights: Small panes of glass set into causes (lead strips) to form a window.

linen press: A two-part case piece for the storage of linen, the upper part with doors enclosing shelves or sliding trays, the lower with drawers. An eighteenth- and nineteenth-century form.

lintel: A supporting wood or stone beam across the top of an opening such as that of a door or window.

loggia: A pillared gallery that is open on one side.

logwood: A dyestuff; wood or sawdust from a tree that grows in Central America and the West Indies, used to make a blue, black, or gray color.

lopers: The decorative handholds that front the sliding support rails of a fall-front desk.

louver: One of a series of overlapping slats (for example, in window shutters).

low dresser: A dresser made without a plate rack.

lug pole: Long pole the width of a chimney made of green wood or iron, from which pots and kettles were hung.

lunette: A semicircular opening, as in a lunette window.

luster glass: An iridescent glass, of the type made by Tiffany in the United States.

mansard roof: A roof with two slopes, the lower one steeper to allow extra roof space for the attic rooms.

mantel: The frame surrounding a fireplace; often used to denote just the shelf (mantel shelf).

marrow scoop (or spoon): A utensil with a long, narrow scoop at both ends. Used for extracting marrow from bones.

millinet wire: Fine wire that was used in bonnet making.

molding: A band of wood, either projecting or incised, that has been shaped by a molding plane.

ogee curve: An S-shaped or reverse curve; similar to a cyma curve.

one-drawer stand: A small four-legged table with drawer. A form of the late eighteenth and nineteenth centuries.

order: In classical architecture, a particular style of column and entablature, each with its own distinctive proportions and detailing. The five orders: Doric, Ionic, Corinthian, Tuscan, and Composite. The first three are derived from ancient Greek architecture; Tuscan and Composite are Roman adaptations of the earlier Greek models.

oriel: A bay window located on an upper floor.

ormolu: Gilded bronze or brass made in imitation of gold and often used for furniture mounts.

outshot: A projection of, or an addition to, a building.

overmantel: A decorative treatment above a fireplace, often incorporating a painting or a mirror.

pad foot: A simple rounded or oval-shaped carved foot.

palisade: A strong wooden fence.

Palladian: An interpretation of the classical style developed by Italian architect Andrea Palladio (1508–1580).

parapet: A low wall placed to protect any spot where there is a sudden drop; for example, at the edge of a balcony or housetop.

patina: Surface texture and color acquired over time from general use and exposure.

pattern book: A book of designs for architectural details based on the revived principles of Classical architecture.

pedestal table: A table supported by a central column, commonly leading to a tripod base.

pediment: An ornamental triangular top across a portico, door, window, or piece of furniture; any similar triangular decorative piece over a doorway, fireplace, or other feature. A pediment that is open on top is called a broken pediment.

peel: A flat wooden shovel with a long handle, used to insert bread and pies into the oven, and also remove them from the oven.

Pembroke table: A small table with two drop leaves on its long side and a drawer. Named for the Countess of Pembroke, who ordered the first one made.

pendant: An ornament hanging down from an arch, ceiling, or roof.

pent roof: A narrow roof sloping in one direction.

perry: Fermented pear juice.

piazza: A broad veranda along one or more sides of a house.

piecrust table: A common term used to describe a circular tilt-top tea table or candle stand with a scalloped, molded edge. It was set on a single leg with three feet.

pier table: A side table, often placed in a dining room or parlor, under a mirror or between two windows (the architectural term for that wall space is pier).

pilaster: A flat rectangular column that projects in low relief from a wall or piece of furniture.

pitch: The angle or steepness of a roof.

plinth: A square block at the base of a column that serves as a base for a statue, vase, or finial.

porringer: A small metal bowl often used to serve children.

porte cochere: A porch wide enough to allow access for a vehicle such as a carriage.

portico: A roofed entrance porch, usually with columns.

post-and-beam construction: A system of framing where heavy timber posts and beams are used.

pot hook: Tool to aid lifting and moving pots, especially hot ones.

press cupboard: A fully enclosed cupboard used for domestic storage from the sixteenth century onward.

purlin: Horizontal roof beams used to support roof rafters.

Queen Anne: The style period from 1700–1730, characterized by the introduction of the cabriole leg and sinuous curves.

quoin: A rectangle of stone, wood, or brick used in vertical series to decorate corners of buildings.

rafter: One of a series of parallel sloping roof members designed to support the roof. The rafters of a flat roof are often called joists.

rail: A horizontal framing member that extends from one vertical support to another, as in the crest of a chair.

rat tail: A tapering ridge found on a spoon, running from the base of the handle to the midpoint on the back of the bowl. Serves as reinforcement and decoration. Spoons featured rat tails from about 1670–1720 and were made in silver and pewter.

rat-tail hinge: A hand-wrought door hinge featuring a heart-shaped terminal with a curled or winding tip that resembles a rat's tail.

rebate or rabbet: A channel or groove cut into a surface edge (usually of wood) to receive another piece.

reeding: Convex vertical carving; the reverse of fluting.

refectory table: A long, narrow table made in the seventeenth century. The earliest form of dining table.

Regency: The style period from 1810–1825. The last of the Georgian styles.

retaining wall: Any wall subjected to lateral pressure such as from a bank of earth.

rose blanket: A white woolen blanket embroidered with a geometric "rose"; these blankets were commonly sold in country stores.

rose-head nail: A hand-forged nail used in America during the seventeenth and eighteenth centuries; it has an irregularly shaped, slightly raised head that roughly resembles an open rose.

runit bags (or runnet or rennet bags)**:** The lining membrane of a calf's stomach. Rennet is an enzyme necessary to curdle the milk that is found in the stomach of an unweaned calf.

rustication: The rough finish, made by deep chiseling, given to projecting wood or stonework in a building. The edges or margins were left smooth.

"salted our creatures": Term that means to "feed salt to the animals."

sash window: A window formed with glazed wooden frames that slide up and down in grooves by means of counterbalanced weights. The standard form has two movable sashes and is called a "double-hung sash."

scalding tub: A large tub used to scald animals after slaughtering.

sconce: A wall bracket for holding a light, particularly candles.

scroll: A decorative motif in the shape of the letter S.

scroll pediment: A trade term used to describe a broken-arch pediment.

secretary-bookcase: *see* desk and bookcase

serving spoon: A long spoon (approximately nine inches long) used for serving food at the table.

settee (also called sofa): A seat for two or more people with upholstered back and seat.

settle: A bench seat with a tall, solid back used from the seventeenth to the nineteenth centuries to ward off drafts. Often used near a hearth.

sewing table (also called work table): A small table, usually of high quality, fitted with drawers to hold material and needlework tools.

Sheraton: The style period from 1790–1805, named after the author of *Cabinetmaker's and Upholsterer's Drawing Book*, published in four parts from 1791–94, which established what came to be known as the federal style in America.

shingle: A thin piece of wood or other material, used to cover the roof and walls of a house. Shingles are laid in overlapping rows.

shocks: Sheaves or bundles of grain placed standing up with the cut ends down.

shoe: A horizontal molded piece of wood attached to a chair's rail at the bottom of the back, into which the splat is fitted.

side chair: A dining chair without arms.

sleigh bed: A bed with a curved head- and foot-board that resembles a sleigh.

sleighshoe: An iron plate that is nailed to the bottom of the runner of a sleigh.

slip seat: A removable chair seat, made of cane, rush, or upholstery, that is designed to rest in the four seat rails of a chair.

snuffer: A tool for trimming wicks.

soffit: The underside of a beam, arch, or other architectural element; also, the reveal of the head of a door or window.

soup ladle: A large-bowled utensil with a long and arched handle, used to serve soup at the table.

spindle: A slender, decorative turned piece of wood, similar to a baluster, often used on chair backs.

spit: A long rod to stick through a piece of meat in order to cook it.

splat: The center support in back of a chair, often elegantly shaped and decorated.

stepped gable: The gable end of a building that is constructed with a series of steps along the roof slope but independent of it.

stiles: Upright vertical side supports in a chair back that support the crest rail.

strainer spoon: A large spoon with a strainer in the middle of the bowl, used for straining soups or stews.

stretcher: A horizontal bracing member set between the legs of a chair, table, or the like for added strength and stability.

stringing: A narrow line of decorative inlay set into a contrasting primary wood on furniture.

stucco: A fine cement or plaster used on the surface of walls, moldings, and other decorative architectural elements. By the nineteenth century, stucco was generally used as a term for exterior rendering.

studs: The upright timbers in a timber-framed building.

stuffing spoon (also called basting spoon): A long-handled spoon (at least twelve inches long).

style period: Refers to the forms fashionable in a particular period, usually identified by the monarch (such as Georgian) or designer (such as Chippendale).

summer beam: A principal rafter or load-bearing beam, usually spanning the width of a room.

swing-leg table: A drop-leaf table without stretchers whose leaves are supported by legs that swing out from the frame only.

tall chest: A one-part case piece with five, six, or seven levels of drawers.

terra-cotta: Unglazed, fired clay used for tiles, decorative architectural elements, garden pots, and so on.

tester: The canopy over a four-poster bed, originally made of wood; made of fabric by the eighteenth century.

tie beam: A horizontal timber beam so situated that it ties the principal rafters of a roof together and prevents them from thrusting out of line.

tilt-top table: A pedestal table fitted with a birdcage mechanism or block beneath the top that allows it to tilt when not in use.

tin-kitchen: A kitchen appliance made of tin, used to cook small quantities in front of an open fire; a reflector oven.

tinder-box: A box for holding tinder, flint, and steel for starting a fire.

toleware: A term of French derivation for paint-decorated tinware.

torchere: A tall stand with a very small top that is intended to hold a candlestick, lamp, or decorative object.

tow: The short and coarse fibers of the flax plant, often used to make a coarse cloth; the long fibers from the flax plant are used to make linen.

tracery: A pattern of intersecting bars or a plate with leaflike decoration in the upper part of a Gothic window.

transom: The horizontal member across the top of a door, or across the top or middle of a window.

trencher: A piece of wood, hollowed out, for holding food.

trompe l'oeil: A decorative effect, such as a painting of an architectural detail or a vista, that gives the illusion of reality.

trundle bed (or truckle bed): A low bed on wheels that was kept under a large bed and trundled out at night for use; probably used by children.

truss: A wooden framework in the shape of a bridge or large bracket, used to support timbers, such as those in a roof.

turnings: Furniture elements, such as balusters and spindles, that have been shaped on a lathe.

tympanum: The recessed front-facing board contained within the upper and lower cornices of a pediment.

underbed: A firm under-mattress, often made of straw or corn husks. A featherbed rests on top of the underbed.

veneer: A thin slice of wood used as a surface covering on a base, or less expensive wood, to give it a finished appearance.

veranda: A large porch along one or more sides of a house.

vernacular: A term describing rural architecture built to suit a specific locality, with little stylistic pretension.

vestibule: A passage, hall, or chamber immediately between the outer door and the inside of a building.

viga: A beam that supports the roof in Indian- and Spanish-type dwellings.

volutes: In classical architecture, spiral scrolls, most characteristically forming the capital of a Greek Ionic column; scroll-shaped brackets.

wainscot: The simple, early form of wood paneling, either full height or on the lower half of a wall.

wainscot chair: An impressive armchair, usually profusely carved with crests and ears, named after wainscot oak, which was often imported from Denmark for paneling. A sixteenth- and seventeenth-century form revived in the nineteenth century.

warming pan: A covered pan with a long handle for holding hot coals. Warming pans were inserted in between the sheets to warm the bed before someone got in.

washstand: A small stand designed to hold a wash basin, a pitcher or bottle of water, and beakers.

wattle and daub: Interlaced sticks roughly plastered with a mixture of clay and chopped straw; sometimes horsehair was used as a binding agent.

whortleberries: blueberries

widow's walk: A rooftop platform or narrow walkway, often used as a lookout for ships on eighteenth- and nineteenth-century New England coastal houses.

William & Mary: The style period at the end of the seventeenth century (1680–1700) referring to the reign of William of Orange and Queen Mary, who brought Dutch and Continental tastes to England.

Windsor chair: A chair with a solid seat into which the splayed legs and members of the back (spindles) are wedged. An eighteenth- and nineteenth-century form.

wing chair: *see* easy chair

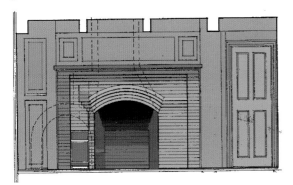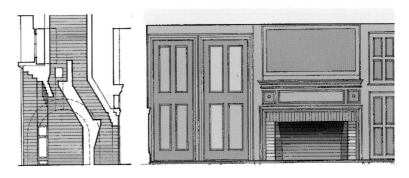

Drawings of the large kitchen fireplace and smaller parlor fireplace flank the section drawing of the chimney stack that serves them both at the historic Buck House in West Chatham, Massachusetts.

Bibliography

Abbott, Jacob. *New England and Her Institutions: By One of Her Sons.* Boston: R. B. Seeley and W. Burnside, 1835.

Abbott, John. *The Mother at Home; or, Principles of Maternal Familiarity Illustrated.* Boston: Crocker & Brewster, 1833.

Abell, Mrs. L. G. *The Skillful Housewife's Book; or, Complete Guide to Domestic Cookery, Taste, Comfort and Economy.* New York: D. Newell, 1846.

Adams, Hannah. *A Memoir of Miss Hannah Adams, Written by Herself with Additional Notices by a Friend.* Boston: Gray and Bowen, 1832.

Allen, Horace L. *The American Farm and Home Cyclopedia.* Indianapolis: Davis and Curtis, 1881.

Allen, Lewis Falley. *Rural Architecture.* New York: Orange Judd, 1852.

The American Farmer's Hand-Book: An Improved and Complete Guide (2nd ed.). Worcester, Mass.: Edward Livermore, 1851.

Arr, E. H. [Ellen Chapman (Hobbs) Rollins]. *New England Bygones.* Philadelphia: J. B. Lippincott, 1880.

Atkeson, Mary Meek. *The Woman on the Farm.* New York and London: The Century Co., 1924.

Atkeson, Thomas C., and Mary Meek Atkeson. *Pioneering in Agriculture.* New York: Orange Judd, 1937.

Bailey, Liberty Hyde. *The Country Life Movement.* New York: Macmillan, 1911.

Bailey, Liberty Hyde, ed. *Cyclopedia of American Agriculture.* New York: Macmillan, 1907–1909.

Barnes, Emily R. *Narratives, Traditions and Personal Reminiscences.* Boston: G. H. Ellis, 1888.

Beam, Lura. *A Maine Hamlet.* New York: Wilfred Funk, 1957.

Beecher, Catherine, and Harriet Beecher Stowe. *The American Woman's Home.* New York: J. B. Ford and Company, 1869.
____. *Treatise on Domestic Economy.* Boston: Marsh, Capen, Lyon and Webb, 1848.

Beecher, Catherine. *Miss Beecher's Domestic Receipt Book.* New York: Harper, 1846.

Beecher, Henry Ward. *Norwood; or Village Life in New England.* New York: Scribner, 1869.

Benjamin, Asher. *American Builder's Companion. 1806.* Rev. 6th ed. Charlestown, Mass., 1811. Reprint, New York: Dover Publications, 1971.

Bevier, Isabel. *The House.* Chicago: American School of Home Economics, 1907.

Bicknell, Amos J. *Wooden and Brick Buildings with Details* (2 vol.). New York: A. J. Bicknell, 1875.

Blake, John Lauris. *The Farmer's Every-day Book.* Auburn, N.Y.: Derby, Miller, & Co., 1851.

Bok, Edward. *The Americanization of Edward Bok.* New York: Scribner, 1920.

Bordley, John Beale. *Essays and Notes on Husbandry and Rural Affairs.* Philadelphia: Thomas Dobson, 1799.

Bremer, Frederika. *The Homes of the New World.* New York: Harper and Brothers, 1868.

Brown, Alice. *The County Road.* 1906. Reprint, Ridgewood, N.J.: Gregg Press, 1968.

Brown, Harriet Connor. *Grandmother Brown's Hundred Years, 1827–1927.* Boston: Little, Brown, 1929.

Brown, Sanborn C. *Benjamin Thompson, Count Rumford.* Cambridge: M.I.T. Press, 1979.

Brunskill, Ronald W. *Illustrated Handbook of Vernacular Architecture.* New York: Universe, 1970.
____. *Traditional Buildings of Britain.* London: Victor Gollancz, 1982.

Bryant, Blanche B., and Gertrude E. Baker, eds. *The Diaries of Sally and Pamela Brown, 1832–1838.* Hyde Leslie 1887. Springfield, Vt.: William L. Bryant Foundation, 1970.

Bud, Jesse. *The Farmer's Companion.* Boston: Marsh, Capen, Lyon and Webb, 1839.

Buell, Joy Day, and Richard Buell, Jr. *The Way of Duty: A Woman and Her Family in Revolutionary America.* New York: Norton, 1984.

Carson, Barbara. *Ambitious Appetites: Dining, Behavior, and Patterns of Consumption in Federal Washington.* Washington, D.C.: American Institute of Architects Press, 1990.

Child, Lydia Maria. *The American Frugal Housewife.* Boston: Carter, Hendee and Company, 1832. Reprint: Worthington, Ohio: Worthington Historical Group, 1965.
____. *The Girl's Own Book.* New York: Clark, Austin and Company, 1833.
____. *The Mother's Book.* Boston: Carter, Hendee, & Babcock, 1831.

Clark, Charles E. *The Eastern Frontier: The Settlement of Northern New England.* New York: Knopf, 1970.

Cleaveland, Henry. *Village and Farm Cottages.* New York: Appleton, 1856.

Cohen, David Steven. *The Dutch-American Farm.* New York: New York University Press, 1992.

Connally, Ernest Allen. *The Cape Cod House: An Introductory Study.* Society of Architectural Historians, 1960.

Cook, Clarence, ed. *A Girl's Life Eighty Years Ago: Letters of Eliza Southgate Bowne.* New York: Scribner, 1883.

Copeland, Robert Morris. *Country Life* (5th ed.). Boston: Dinsmoor & Co., 1866.

Copley, Esther. *Cottage Comforts.* London: Simpkin and Marshall, 1836.

Cott, Nancy. *The Bonds of Womanhood: "Woman's Sphere" in New England, 1780–1835.* New Haven: Yale University Press, 1977.

Crow, Martha Foote. *The American Country Girl.* New York: Frederick A. Stokes, 1915.

Cummings, Abbott Lowell, comp. *Bed Hangings: A Treatise on Fabrics and Styles in the Curtaining of Beds, 1650–1850.* Boston: Society for the Preservation of New England Antiquities, 1961.
____. *Rural Household Inventories.* Boston: Society for the Preservation of New England Antiquities, 1964.

Deetz, James. *In Small Things Forgotten.* New York: Anchor Books, Doubleday, 1996.

Denenberg, Thomas Andrew. *Wallace Nutting and the Invention of America.* New Haven and London: Yale University Press, 2003.

Dodd, Helen. *The Healthful Farmhouse* (2nd ed.). Boston: Whitcomb and Barrow, 1911.

Dow, George Francis. *The Arts and Crafts in New England, 1704–1775.* Topsfield, Mass.: Wayside Press, 1927.

Downing, Andrew Jackson. *The Architecture of Country Houses*. 1850. Reprint, New York: Dover Publications, 1969.

____. *Cottage Residences*. 1842. Reprint, Watkins Glen, N.Y.: American Life Foundation, 1967.

____. *Hints to Persons About Building in the Country*. New York: John Wiley, 1851.

____. *Rural Essays*. New York: G. P. Putnam, 1853.

Earle, Alice Morse. *Home Life in Colonial Days*. New York: The Macmillan Company, 1898.

Eastman, Edward R. *Journey to Day Before Yesterday*. Englewood Cliffs, N.J.: Prentice-Hall, 1963.

Erickson, Theodore. *My 60 Years With Rural Youth*. Minneapolis: University of Minnesota Press, 1956.

Fegley, H. Winslow. *Farming, Always Farming*. Birdsboro, Pa.: The Pennsylvania German Society, 1987.

Fletcher, Stevenson Whitcomb. *Pennsylvania Agriculture and Country Life, 1640–1840*. Harrisburg, Pa.: Pennsylvania Historical and Museum Commission, 1950.

Gardner, E. C. *Homes and How to Make Them*. Boston: J. R. Osgood, 1874.

Garrett, Elisabeth Donaghy. *At Home: The American Family, 1750–1870*. New York: Harry N. Abrams, 1990.

Glassie, Henry. *Pattern in the Material Folk Culture of the Eastern United States*. Philadelphia: University of Pennsylvania Press, 1971.

Goodale, Elaine. [Elaine Goodale Eastman). *Journal of a Farmer's Daughter*. New York: G. P. Putnam's Sons, 1881.

Hawke, David Freeman. *Everyday Life in Early America*. New York: Harper and Row, 1988.

Howard, Hugh. *How Old Is This House?*. New York: The Noonday Press, Farrar, Straus and Giroux, 1989.

____. *House Dreams*. Chapel Hill, N.C.: Algonquin Books, 2001.

Howland, Mrs. E. A. *The New England Economical Housekeeper and Family Receipt Book*. Worcester, Mass.: S. A. Howland, 1845.

Hubka, Thomas C. *Big House, Little House, Back House, Barn*. Hanover, N.H.:University Press of New England, 1984.

Jackle, John A., Robert W. Bastian, and Douglas K. Meyer, *Common Houses in America's Small Towns*. Athens, Ga.: The University of Georgia Press, 1989.

Jewett, Sarah Orne. *Country By-Ways*. Boston: Houghton, Mifflin and Company, 1888.

Jones, Alice Hanson. *American Colonial Wealth: Documents and Methods* (3 vols.). New York: Arno Press, 1977.

Kauffman, Henry J. *The American Farmhouse*. New York: Hawthorn Books, 1979.

King, Caroline Howard. *When I Lived in Salem, 1822–1866*. Brattleboro, Vt.: Stephen Day Press, 1937.

Kunstler, James Howard. *The Geography of Nowhere*. New York: A Touchstone Book, Simon and Schuster, 1994.

____. *Home from Nowhere*. New York: A Touchstone Book, Simon and Schuster, 1998.

Larcom, Lucy. *A New England Girlhood*. Boston: Houghton, Mifflin and Company, 1889.

Larkin, Jack. *The Reshaping of Everyday Life*. Sturbridge, Mass.: Old Sturbridge Village, 1987.

Lee, Eliza Buckminster. *Sketches of a New England Village in the Last Century*. Boston: James Munroe and Company, 1838.

Leland, E. H. *Farm Homes: In-Doors and Out-Doors*. New York: Orange Judd, 1881.

Lesley, Susan I. *Recollections of My Mother, Anne Jean Lyman of Northampton*. Boston: Houghton, Mifflin and Company, 1899.

Leslie, Eliza. *The House Book*. Philadelphia: Carey and Hart, 1841.

Little, William. *The History of Warren: A Mountain Hamlet, Located among the White Hills of New Hampshire*. Manchester, N.H.: W. E. Moore, 1870.

Livermore, Mary. *The Story of My Life*. Hartford, Conn.: 1899.

Long, Amos, Jr. *The Pennsylvania German Family Farm*. Brienigsville, Pa.: The Pennsylvania German Society, 1972.

Lyman, Laura, and Joseph Bardwell Lyman. *The Household Guide and Philosophy of Housekeeping* (14th ed.).

Hartford, Conn.: James Betts, 1869.

Martin, Glenna. *"Just a Housewife": The Rise and Fall of Domesticity in America*. New York: Oxford University Press, 1987.

Mason, Francis, ed. *Childish Things: The Reminiscence of Susan Baker Blunt*. Grantham, N.H.: Tompson and Rutter, 1988.

Mayer, Lance, and Guy Myers. *The Devotion Family: The Lives and Personal Possessions of Three Generations in Eighteenth-Century Connecticut*. New London, Conn.: Lyman Allen Museum, 1991.

Mayhew, Edgar, and Minor Myers, Jr. *A Documentary History of American Interiors from the Colonial Era to 1915*. New York: Scribner, 1980.

McKeever, William A. *Farm Boys and Girls*. New York: Macmillan, 1913.

McMurry, Sally. *Families and Farmhouses in Nineteenth-Century America: Vernacular Design and Social Change*. New York: Oxford University Press, 1988.

Mitchell, Donald Grant. *My Farm of Edgewood*. New York: Charles Scribner, 1863.

Mitchell, Stewart, ed. *New Letters of Abigail Adams, 1788–1801*. Boston: Houghton Mifflin Company, 1947.

Morgan, Edmund S. *The Puritan Family*. New York: Harper and Row, 1966.

Morris, Edmund. *Farming for Boys*. Boston: Ticknor & Fields, 1868.

Morrison, Hugh. *Early American Architecture*. New York: Oxford University Press, 1952.

Mussey, Barrows, ed. *Yankee Life by Those Who Lived It*. New York: Alfred A. Knopf, 1947.

Nash, John Adams. *The Progressive Farmer*. New York: A. O. Moore, 1857.

Nylander, Jane C. *Our Own Snug Fireside: Images of the New England Home, 1760–1860*. New York: Knopf, 1993.

Sklar, Kathryn Kish. *Catherine Beecher: A Study in American Domestic Economy*. New Haven and London: Yale University Press, 1973.

Sloat, Caroline, ed. *The Old Sturbridge Village Cookbook*. Chester, Conn.: Globe Pequot Press, 1984.

Sneller, Ann Gertrude. *A Vanished World*. Syracuse, N.Y.: Syracuse University Press, 1964.

Stephens, Henry. *The Book of the Farm* (2 vols.). New York: Greeley & McElrath, 1847.

Stevens, John Calvin, and Albert W. Cobb. *Examples of American Domestic Architecture*. New York: William Comstock, 1889.

Stowe, Harriet Beecher. *House and Home Papers*. Boston: Ticknor and Fields, 1865.
_____. *Oldtown Folks*. Boston: Fields, Osgood, 1869.

Strasser, Susan. *Never Done: A History of American Housework*. New York: Pantheon Books, 1982.

Todd, Sereno Edwards. *Todd's Country Home and How to Save Money*. Hartford, Conn.: Hartford Publishing Co., 1870.

Tuthill, Louisa C. *The Nursery Book*. New York: G. P. Putnam, 1849.
_____. *The Young Lady's Home*. Boston: William J. Reynolds, 1847.

Ulrich, Laurel Thatcher. *Good Wives: Image and Reality in the Lives of Women in Northern New England, 1650–1750*. New York: Knopf, 1982.

Underwood, Francis. *Quabbin: The Story of a New England Town*. Boston: Lee & Shepard, 1893.

Upton, Dell, ed. *America's Architectural Roots: Ethnic Groups That Built America*. Washington, D.C.: The Preservation Press, 1986.

Upton, Dell, and John Michael Vlach, eds. *Common Places: Readings in American Vernacular Architecture*. Athens, Ga.: University of Georgia Press, 1986.

Van Rensselaer, Martha, et al. *A Manual of Homemaking*. New York: Macmillan, 1919.

Van Wagenen, Jared, Jr. *Days of My Years*. Cooperstown: New York State Historical Association, 1962.

Vanderbilt, Gertrude Lefferts. *The Social History of Flatbush*. New York: Frederick Loeser and Co., 1909.

Varney, Almon C. *Our Homes and Their Adornments*. Chicago: People's Publishing Co., 1885.

Vaux, Calvert. *Villas and Cottages*. 1864. Reprint, New York: Dover Publications, 1970.

Webster, Thomas, and Mrs. William Parkes. *An Encyclopaedia of Domestic Economy*. New York: Harper and Brothers, 1848.

Wheeler, Gervase. *Homes for the People*. rev. ed. New York: The American News Co., 1867.

Williams, Henry T., and Mrs. S. C. Jones. *Beautiful Homes*. New York: Henry T. Williams, 1877.

Articles

Marshall, Howard Wight. *Vernacular Architecture in Rural and Small Town Missouri*. Columbia, Mo.: Extension Publications, 1994.

Umphrey, Michael. *Foodways in 1910*. Montana Heritage Project.

Women of the West Museum. *There Are No Renters Here—Homesteading in a Sod House*. Nebraska State Historical Society.

Old Sturbridge Village Teacher Resources: *Historical Background on the 19th Century Farm Family.
A Summer Day.
Asa Sheldon's Boyhood.
Housekeeping Advice.
Mary Livermore's Childhood Kitchen*

Periodicals

American Agriculturist. 1841-
Cultivator. 1834–.
Ohio Farmer. 1858-
Prairie Farmer. 1841-
Rural Affairs. 1855-.

Opposite: *An abandoned federal farmhouse in New York.*

Acknowledgments

I would like to thank the following for their help in the preparation of this book:

Craig Becker, Rebecca Bell, Belton Masonry, Mark Bilak, Jim Buckley, Madelyn Ewing, Wendell Garrett, The Gibbs Museum of Pioneer and Dakota Life, Alexander Greenwood, Lynn Karlin, Russell Keegan, Kline Creek Farm, Tricia Levi, Chris Miller, Montana Heritage Project, Ellen Nidy, Robert Robinson, and Jeff Schonberg

Special thanks are due to Elric Endersby for the use of his library of books on rural architecture and history, and Gladys Montgomery Jones for allowing me to use her writings on paints and wall coverings. The books by David Steven Cohen, Elizabeth Donaghy Garrett, Sally McMurry, and Jane C. Nylander, and the articles by Steven Mintz and Michael Umphrey are in my opinion the best of their kind in describing the history of farmhouse and domestic work. Old Sturbridge Village Teaching Resources on farm family life with their articles, diaries, and excerpts from historic books were extremely helpful.

Photo credits

Craig Becker: 2, 115. Solomon Butcher Collection: 52 *middle right, bottom right.* Case Ranch: 188, 189, 192, *bottom left.* DeHaven: 190 *top left.* Madelyn Ewing: 182 *left top, bottom, and near right top,* 183, *top left and right.* Michael Freeman: 19, 19 *margin,* 20 *left and right,* 24 *top left,* 25 *top and bottom,* 50, 51, 60-61, 62, 63, 65, 68-69, 70, 71, 74, 75, 90, 117, 130. Historic American Buildings Survey: 36, 46, 47 *left,* 49 *right,* 52 *top.* Howard Creek Ranch: 190 *bottom right,* 191. Gladys Montgomery Jones: 198, 223. Lynn Karlin: 182 *top right, bottom right,* 183 *bottom left and right,* 184, 185. Kline Farm: 186, 187. David Larkin: 11, 15, 18, 26 *top left and right,* 32, 41, 202, 203, 224. The Inn at Locke House: 197. The Magazine Antiques: 27. Palo Alto Creek Farm: 192 *bottom right,* 193 *top left.* Paul Rocheleau: 6-7, 12, 16, 19 *bottom right,* 23, 24 *bottom left,* 28-29, 30-31, 34, 37, 38, 43, 44 *top and bottom,* 48-49, 53, 55, 57, 58, 60, 72-73, 77, 78, 79, 80, 82-83, 84, 85, 88-89, 101, 103, 104-105, 108, 110, 112, 118-119, 122, 123, 125, 127, 129, 132 *top left,* 134-135, 136, 137, 138-139, 148, 149, 150, 151, 152, 153, 199. Sakura Ridge: 193 *bottom,* 194. Jeff Schonberg: 101 *margin.* Carl Socolow: 13, 17, 66, 82 *top,* 106, 142, 143, 200. Jessie Walker: 45, 47 *right,* 87, 91, 92, 93, 94, 95 97, 98, 107, 109, 111, 113, 120, 121, 126, 131, 132 *bottom left,* 133, 140-141, 144, 145, 146, 147, 154, 155, 156, 157, 158, 159, 160, 161, 162, 163, 164, 165, 166, 167, 168, 169, 170, 171, 172, 173, 174, 175, 176, 177, 178, 179, 180, 181, 195, 196, 205.